PEOPLE OF INDIA

DADRA
AND
NAGAR HAVELI

Volume XVIII

PEOPLE OF INDIA

NATIONAL SERIES

VOL. I	PEOPLE OF INDIA	AN INTRODUCTION
VOL. II	PEOPLE OF INDIA	THE SCHEDULED CASTES
VOL. III	PEOPLE OF INDIA	THE SCHEDULED TRIBES
VOL. IV	PEOPLE OF INDIA	ALL COMMUNITIES
VOL. V	PEOPLE OF INDIA	ALL COMMUNITIES
VOL. VI	PEOPLE OF INDIA	ALL COMMUNITIES
VOL. VII	PEOPLE OF INDIA	IDENTITY, ECOLOGY, SOCIAL ORGANIZATION ECONOMY, DEVELOPMENT PROCESS AND LINKAGES: A QUANTITATIVE PROFILE
VOL. VIII	PEOPLE OF INDIA	COMMUNITIES, SEGMENTS, SYNONYMS, SURNAMES AND TITLES
VOL. IX	PEOPLE OF INDIA	LANGUAGES AND SCRIPTS
VOL. X	PEOPLE OF INDIA	THE BIOLOGICAL VARIATION IN INDIAN POPULATIONS
VOL. XI	PEOPLE OF INDIA	AN ANTHROPOLOGICAL ATLAS

STATES SERIES

VOL. XII	ANDAMAN AND NICOBAR ISLANDS
VOL. XIII	ANDHRA PRADESH
VOL. XIV	ARUNACHAL PRADESH
VOL.XV	ASSAM
VOL.XVI	BIHAR
VOL.XVII	CHANDIGARH
VOL.XVIII	DADRA AND NAGAR HAVELI
VOL.XIX	DAMAN AND DIU
VOL.XX	DELHI
VOL.XXI	GOA
VOL.XXII	GUJARAT
VOL.XXIII	HARYANA
VOL.XXIV	HIMACHAL PRADESH
VOL.XXV	JAMMU AND KASHMIR
VOL.XXVI	KARNATAKA
VOL.XXVII	KERALA
VOL.XXVIII	LAKSHADWEEP
VOL.XXIX	MADHYA PRADESH
VOL.XXX	MAHARASHTRA
VOL.XXXI	MANIPUR
VOL.XXXII	MEGHALAYA
VOL.XXXIII	MIZORAM
VOL.XXXIV	NAGALAND
VOL.XXXV	ORISSA
VOL.XXXVI	PONDICHERRY
VOL.XXXVII	PUNJAB
VOL.XXXVIII	RAJASTHAN
VOL.XXXIX	SIKKIM
VOL.XL	TAMIL NADU
VOL.XLI	TRIPURA
VOL.XLII	UTTAR PRADESH
VOL XLIII	WEST BENGAL

PEOPLE OF INDIA

DADRA
AND
NAGAR HAVELI

Volume XVIII

General Editor
K. S. SINGH

Editors
Faquir Chand
N. K. Sinha

ANTHROPOLOGICAL SURVEY OF INDIA
POPULAR PRAKASHAN PVT. LTD.
BOMBAY

POPULAR PRAKASHAN PVT LTD
Bombay

People of India : *Dadra and Nagar Haveli*

First Published 1994

Typeset by PRINTOX, New Delhi
Printed in India at Gopsons Papers (Pvt.) Ltd., A 28, Sector IX
NOIDA
Published by Ramdas Bhatkal for Popular Prakashan Pvt Ltd
35C, Pandit Madan Mohan Malaviya Marg, Tardeo
Bombay-400 034

ISBN 81 - 7154 - 762 - 1

(3534)

CONTENTS

ILLUSTRATIONS

A NOTE ON THE SERIES

There exists an information gap on a very large number of communities in India, and the information that exists on them is scanty or needs to be updated. The Anthropological Survey of India (An.S.I.) launched a project on the People of India on 2nd October 1985. The objective of the project was to generate a brief, descriptive anthropological profile of all the communities of India, the impact on them of change and development processes and the links that bring them together. This was in accordance with the objectives of the An.S.I., established forty-seven years ago in December 1945. The An.S.I. has been pursuing bio-cultural research among different population groups from its eight regional centres. Its objectives have been redefined in the policy resolution adopted in 1985, which commits this organization to the survey of the human surface of India.

The identification of the communities and their listing have had a long history which started from the early period of our history with Manu. Regional lists of communities figured in Sanskrit works. Medieval chronicles contained a description of communities located in various parts of the country. Listings in the colonial period were undertaken on an extensive scale after 1806. The process gathered momentum in course of the censuses from 1881 to 1941. In our compilation of the lists of the communities of India under the People of India project, we drew upon ethnographic surveys, the lists of Scheduled Castes and Scheduled Tribes drawn up by the Government of India, the lists of backward classes prepared by Backward Classes Commissions set up by various State governments, and the list that exists in the Mandal Commission Report. We were able to put together about 6748 communities at the start. This list was taken to the field, tested and checked, and finally 4635 communities were identified and studied.

Unlike surveys in the colonial period, which covered British India and a few princely states, our project covers the whole country, bringing within its ambit such parts that had not been ethnographically surveyed earlier or where the survey had been done in a perfunctory way. Each State and Union Territory was treated as a unit of study. It was decided to start with the investigation of the least-known communities, and then move on to a field study of the lesser-known and better-known ones. Investigators for the survey were identified for each area on the basis of their experience and expertise. Teams of investigators of the Survey, as well as local scholars, were set up for each State and Union Territory to plan the surveys, seek the co-operation of local scholars, generate and evaluate findings, etc. Later, Editorial Boards consisting of local scholars — one or more of these were nominated as Co-Editor/s for each local volume — were set up for each State and Union Territory. We sought the co-operation of the State Governments in implementing the project, and this we received in ample measure, particularly from the Welfare and Backward Classes Departments of the State Governments, local officers of the Census of India, tribal research institutes, university departments of anthropology, other departments of local universities, etc. Local scholars participated enthusiastically in our project as well as in the discussion at seminars held by us.

The progress in the investigation and coverage of communities from 2nd October 1985 to 31st March 1992 was steady and impressive. We were able to identify, locate and study 4635 communities in all the States and Union Territories of India, out of the 6748 listed initially. As many as 600 scholars participated in this project, including 197 from 26 institutions. About 100 workshops and rounds of discussions were held in all the States and Union Territories, and in these about 3000 scholars participated. The investigators spent 26510 days in the field, which works out to 5.5 days per community studied in the various States and Union Territories of India. Our scholars interviewed a large number of people, out of whom we have recorded only the key informants, i.e. 24951. This works out to about five 'informed' informants per community. Of the informants, 4981 were women. Our instruction to the investigators was to study a community at two or three places, and in at least two or three cultural regions into which the larger States of India are divided. Interviews were conducted in connection with the study of the communities in 3581 villages, mostly multi-community villages, and in 1011 towns and cities spread over almost all the districts of India, i.e. 421 districts and 91 cultural regions. We were able, thus, to study on an average a community at about two places. It should be noted that most of the smaller communities could be studied at only one place since they are not located in more than one area.

A major achievement of this project was the preparation of cartographic maps showing the distribution of the communities and the locations where they were studied. About 4000 maps were prepared. Yet another achievement was the visual documentation of the People of India as part of the field operations. About 21,362 photographs were generated, most of them in black and white, and a substantial number in colour, by amateur photographers.

At an early stage of our project in March 1985, we decided to transfer the data to a computer. We were subsequently able to develop probably the first software in the country — and one of the first in the world — in ethnography, in close collaboration with the National Informatics Centre. From 28th May 1988 we started transferring the quantitative data collected in computer format to floppies. Simultaneously, the transfer of descriptive data (abstracts etc.) to the computer also started at almost all the regional centres. We succeeded in computerizing an enormous mass of data, and also in producing the first results of univariate analysis by March 1990.

The descriptive material, running into 120 manuscript volumes, and the quantitative data contained in 257 diskettes, were released on 1st October 1990 by Sri Chimanbhai Mehta, Minister of State for Human Resource Development, in the presence of a distinguished audience in Delhi, for use by scholars at the Nehru Memorial Museum and Library, and at eight Regional Centres of the An.S.I.

The phase of more elaborate analysis started in July 1991 in collaboration with the Centre for Ecological Sciences, Indian Institute of Science, Bangalore. This resulted in a voluminous output of analysed data, which has been presented in a comprehensive matrix consisting of the four categories of populations — the constitutional, religious, occupational and locational. These sets of data, together with a map, were released by Shri Arjun Singh, Minister of Human Resource Development, on 24th December 1991. The last Workshop on the People of India project was held at the Indian Institute of Social and Economic Change in Bangalore, where the preliminary results of the analysis presented by the An.S.I. were discussed by distinguished scholars.

It should be noted that the study of the communities has been conducted in 3581 villages and 1011 towns situated in 421 districts of the States and Union Territories of India. The information was collected from about 25000 of the 'learned' informants by our scholars, 500 of them, over the period 1985 to 1992. Therefore, the observations relate to this limited time frame and to the universe of the ethnographic project titled People of India. The percentages relate strictly to the responses made by the informants to the questionnaire contained in the scheduled guideline and computer format, and to the queries made by the investigators at the places of investigation. The responses have been supplemented with the observations of the investigators, the secondary material from the census, ethnographic records etc. The material has been checked and cross-checked by scholars, particularly local scholars, at many levels with other sources of information.

We are presenting the material published under the People of India project in two parts which are interrelated. The first consists of the ten-volume national series, five of which contain an abstract on all communities across the length and breadth of the country. The data generated in this respect has been strengthened by the addition of information from census and other secondary sources. These volumes include two on the Scheduled Castes and Scheduled Tribes, prepared as part of the celebration of Dr B.R. Ambedkar's Birth Centenary; three on all the communities of India, and two containing data on the languages and biological structures of Indian population. The remaining volumes contain description of the quantitative profile, communities and their segments, community-specific languages and the biological structure of Indian populations.

The second part comprises the State/Union Territory volumes, with detailed descriptive account of each community of India. The contributors to the national volumes on the SC, ST and all communities are listed in the last volume, Volume VI. The Glossary given in Volume VI is common to all the national volumes. At the end of each account, we have given references to the texts from which we have quoted, or references for further reading. This is only illustrative. An exhaustive bibliography appears at the end of the national volumes, in Volume VI.

A consortium of publishers has been set up to publish the material on States and Union Territories. Seven volumes each for the northern States, southern States and the Islands, the central and western States will be published respectively by M/s Manohar Publishers and Distributors (New Delhi), M/s Affiliated East-West

Press Private Limited (Madras) and M/s Popular Prakashan Pvt. Ltd. (Bombay). The eleven volumes on the north-eastern and eastern States will be published by M/s Seagull Books Private Limited (Calcutta), which has already published the introductory national volume, which in its turn will be followed by the other national volumes to be published by the Oxford University Press.

I trust this series on the People of India, which is based on a comprehensive anthropological survey of the country, will be found useful by all sections of our people, including students, researchers, teachers, social activists, administrators and political leaders. I hope we have laid the groundwork for a comprehensive ethnography of the People of India which needs to be continually updated and built upon by successive generations of researchers and scholars.

K. S. Singh

FOREWORD

The fourteen communities of Dadra and Nagar Haveli were identified and studied ethnographically for the first time under the People of India project (POI). No survey of these communities was undertaken in the colonial period. The material collected by Anthropological Survey of India was analysed and discussed at the workshop held in April 91 in Udaipur. Dadra and Nagar Haveli form part of Western Regional Centre of Anthropological Survey of India.

Of these communities studied by us, six are tribals, and one, Chamar, is the scheduled caste. Besides, there is one Muslim community, Makrana. The Parsis with their legendary number of 12,000 had arrived in India and landed at Diu first from where they spread to other parts. They are still a land- owning and trading community. The Rajput community originally came from the North and took shelter in Dharampur state. The Kahars now deal in dry fish. Other communities such as Agari, Kapadia etc. are engaged in business and agriculture. The Bharwad is a pastoral community. The Warli are the autochthones of the region. The tribal population which was 88.5 per cent of the total population (1961), with the influx of non tribals, to 78.82 per cent (1981).

The analysis of the data for these communities in terms of the parameters of the POI project presents an interesting pattern. The socio-cultural system of the territory is only an extension of the larger system prevailing in Gujarat. The communities except four tribal groups who represent an overflow of the populations from Maharashtra have mostly migrated from South Gujarat. Most of them are migrants (86%). There for as many as 12 communities who identify themselves at regional level and one (the Parsi) at national level. Ethnographic accounts are available for most of the communities (71%). They also see their distribution at the regional level. Most of the communities are located in the hilly terrain which has only a thin forest cover left and live in the climate characterised by moderate temperature, high humidity and medium rainfall. Most of the men and women are non-vegetarian and consume mainly rice, wheat, *bajra*, *tur* and gram. Mostly men consume alcoholic drink. The Bharwad produce and distribute milk.

Social divisions particularly in the form of clan organisation have been reported in all the communities. All communities are endogamous. The tribes stand outside of varna system. Consanguineous forms of marriage, of both FSD and MBD types exist in the tribal communities. Junior sororate is widespread (71%). Adult marriage is being increasingly practised (71%). Marriage by negotiation (93%) is the norm. Marriage by service has been reported by four tribal communities. Some tribal groups have reported both sororal and non-sororal polygyny. Junior sororate is also widespread (43%). Interestingly, *tali/mangalsutra* or *ganthi* as it is widely called is used as a symbol of marriage making this region an extension of the southern region particularly Konkan. Payment of brideprice is generally the norm. Dowry in kind rather than in cash has been reported from two communities. The rule of residence is entirely patrilocal. Divorce is permissible in most of the communities for reasons of adultery, witchcraft etc. Remarriage of both widow and widower is permitted in as many as 12 communities. Both extended and nuclear families exist in most of the communities. Male equigeniture is the norm and no property right of the female is reported, in spite of the substantial role played by the women in the economic activities like agriculture, in maintaining household by collecting fuel, fetching potable water etc. The status of women is generally considered low.

The communities are mostly dependent on land (11) and forest (2). Hunting and gathering once reported in the literature has ceased to exist. So has shifting cultivation. Trapping of birds and animals has been reported by one community only, Kathodi. Terrace cultivation is practised by two communities, Kokna and Warli. Most of the communities have settled down to cultivation and work as labourers. There is a concentration of communities who depend on business and trade in local forest produce, merchandise and so on. Most of the communities have reported that a number of their members are engaged in government service(11) and employed as industrial workers (3), non skilled labourers, in skin and hide work and fishing. The Kathodi were brought in by the Parsis for manufacturing country liquor. Bonded labour which once existed has now been abolished. Barter system exists in tribal markets. There is a sharp increase in the number of wage labourers in agriculture and industries. Traditional caste council/tribal council exists universally to ensure social solidarity. Clan deities exist in most of the communities, their worship being an integral part of their social organisation, as do village deities, which are also an integral part of village communities particularly in tribal areas. Since the Portuguese times, conversion to Christianity has been reported among the two communities, Kokna and Warli. The religious movements have penetrated from Gujarat into this area and there are followers of many sects such as Jala Ram, Jai Gurudev, Shanti Panth, Gayatri Pariwar and Swami Narayan. There are strong folk traditions stressed by the popularity of folk literature particularly in tribal areas. While communities are developing commonalities in terms of sharing of water resources, participation in festivals etc., it appears that the old pattern of commensal restrictions still exists except in tribal areas.

There has been a visible impact of the development process on all communities. From the analysis of data it appears that the impact of some of the aspects of development process has been most widespread compared to the rest of the country. However, the gender bias in matter of access to education, employment persists.

Although a small territory, there are speakers of as many as eight languages : Chamari, Dubli, Dhodia, Gujarati, Kokni, Konkani and Varli belonging to Indo-Aryan languages. Makarani is a foreign language and is unclassified. Gujarati language is spoken by the largest number of communities (8) followed by Kokni spoken by two communities (Katkari/Kathodi and Kokna); Konkani is spoken by the Koli Dhor/Kolga/Kolcha community. The other five languages such as Chamari, Dubli, Dhodia, Makrani and Varli are spoken by one community each, the name of the communities being the same as that of the language. According to 1981 census, Gujarati is spoken by 22,031 persons in the Union Territory of Dadra and Nagar Haveli, Konkani by 6,904 persons. Gujarati language is also used for communication. Among the Gujarati speakers, 6,727 persons speak Hindi and 360 persons Bhili. Among the Konkani speakers, 412 persons speak Marathi and 183 persons have claimed Bhili. The Gujarati and the Devanagari scripts are commonly used in the Union Territory of Dadra and Nagar Haveli.

Bio-anthropological information is available only for the Scheduled Tribes. The incidence of colour blindness ranges from 2.35-4.27%. G6PD deficiency is rather high 6.35-19.62%. The Scheduled Tribes show a higher incidence of A gene 18.91-34.20%

than B gene 13.97-22.17%. M gene varies from 34.40-50.37%. R_1 haplotype has a very high frequency 71.40-88.08% and correspondingly r haplotype shows low incidence 0.00-8.80%. P_1 gene (p blood group) and Fy^a gene (Duffy system) vary from 31.10- 47.45% and 56-65% respectively. Hp^1 has a low incidence 8.48 - 13.76%.

K.S.Singh

ACKNOWLEDGEMENT

We are grateful to the Administration of Dadra and Nagar Haveli particularly Shri K.D. Sigh, the then collector, for extending cooperation at all stages of research. Our sincere thanks are also due to Shri Faquir Chand, Deputy Director, Planning and Statistics Department of Daman, Diu, Dadra and Nagar Haveli Administration for going through the reports and making necessary corrections. He is also our co-editor. We also acknowledge the contributions of many friends from Dadra and Nagar Haveli such as Shri O.P. Vyas, Shri S.L. Shah, Statistical Assistant, Miss Nirmala Kamath, Child Welfare and Development Officer, Mrs. Snehlata Balkrishna Mahale, Mukhya Sevika, Shri J.N. Dessai, a freedom fighter and those of the Institutions such as Vanvasi Kalyan Ashram, Khanvel. Acknowledgement is also due to Shri D.S. Hooda, Cartographer, at the North-West Regional Centre, Dehradun for preparing the map and to Mrs. Kum Kum Srivastava, Designer, for preparing the jacket design.

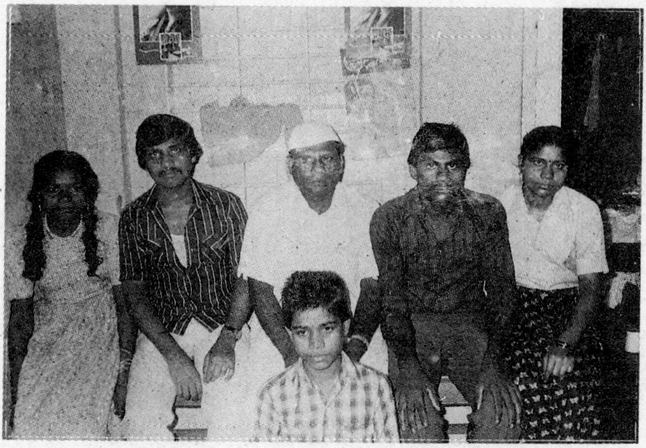

1. An Agri family

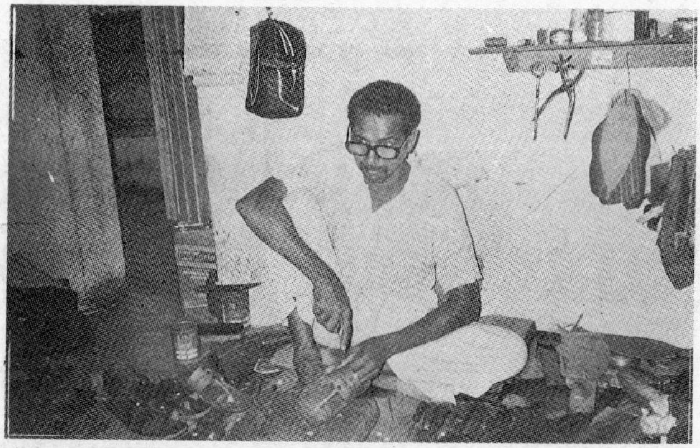

2. A Chamar

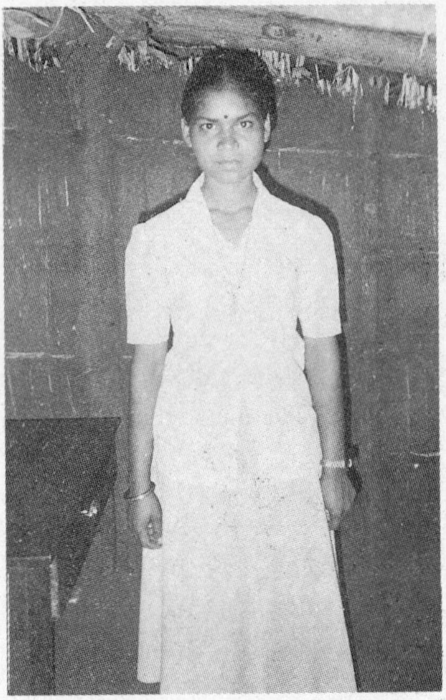

3. A Christian Varli girl

4. A Kahar family

5. A Kapadia family

6. A Kapadia

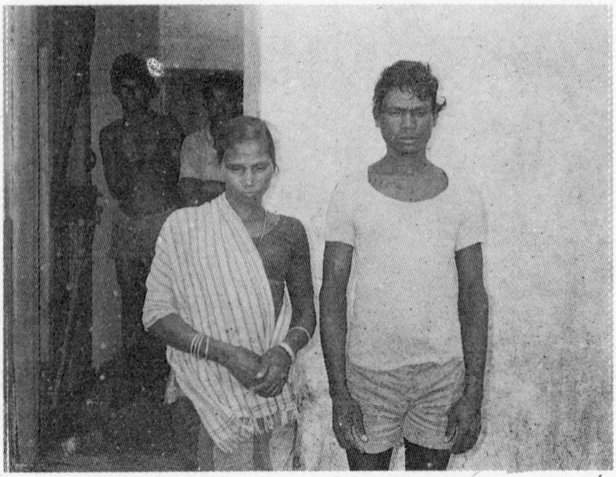

7. A Kathodi couple

8. A Kokna engaged in ploughing

9. A Kokna family engaged in basketry

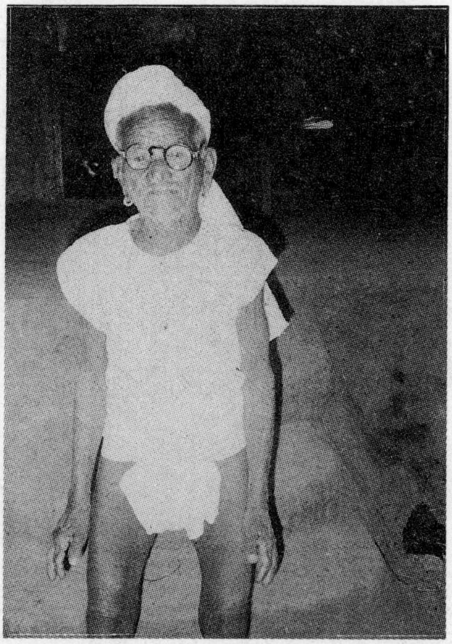

10. A Kokna in traditional dress

11. A Koli Dhor marriage procession

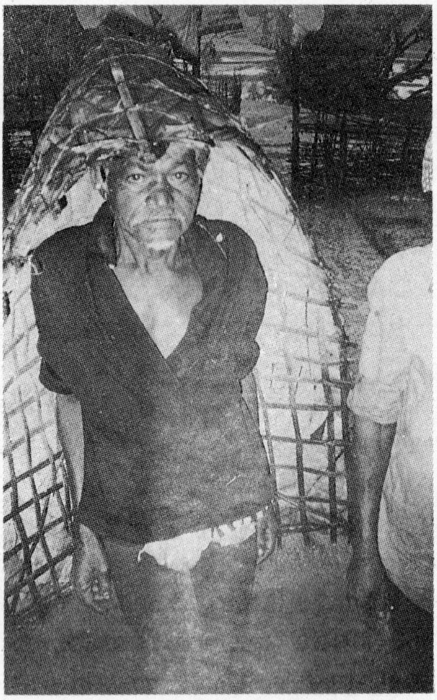

12. A Koli Dhor with
traditional rain coat

13. The Koli Dhor girls

14. The Makrana men

15. Mask used during Bhowada folk dance

16. A Mauri Rajput family

17 A Parsi with traditional headgear

18. A tribal mart

19. A Varli hut

20. The Varli women

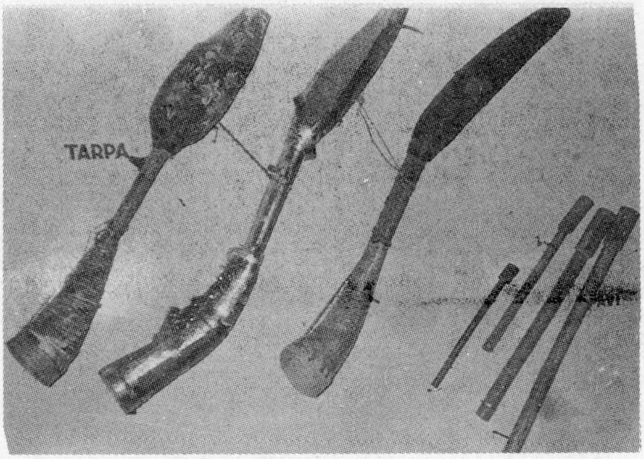

21. Musical instrucments used by the tribals

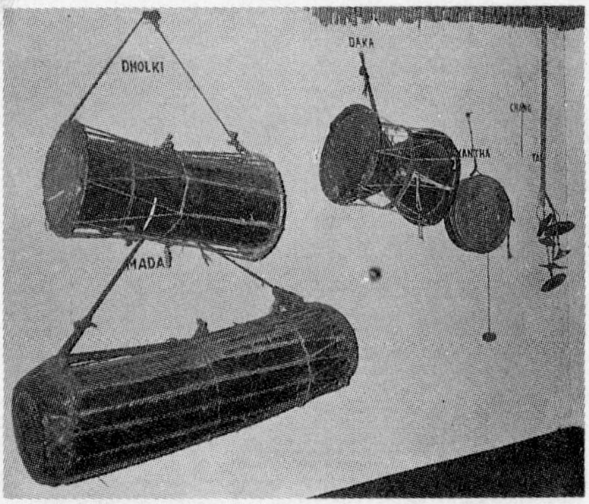

22. Musical instrucments
used by the tribals

INTRODUCTION

Dadra and Nagar Haveli came under the Potugese rule in the late 18th century, and remained under their domain for nearly 170 years. Dadra was liberated on 22 July 1954 while Nagar Haveli was liberated on 2 August1954. Both were brought under the Free Dadra and Nagar Haveli Administration. Subsequently on 11 August 1961, it was constituted as a separate Union Territory. The administrative head of the Union Territory is also the Administrator of Goa, Daman and Diu. The territory comprises two pockets namely Dadra with three villages and Nagar Haveli with 68 villages and one town. Silvasa, the headquarters of the territory, is located between Bombay and Surat and is linked with National Highway No. 8. It is about fifteen kilometers east of Vapi railway station in Gujarat. It is situated on the western coast of India between the parallels of 20°.0' and 20° 25' of North Latitude and between 72° 50' and 73° 15' East Longitude. The total area of the territory according to Census of India 1971 is 489 sq. kms. It is bounded by Umargaon taluka of Valsad district of Gujarat and Dahnu or Dahanu taluka of Thana district of Maharashtra on the west, Pardi and Dharampur talukas of Valsad distsrict on the north, Dahnu taluka of Thana district on the south and Dharamnpur taluka of Valsad district and Jawar taluka of Thana district on the east.

The landscape of Dadra is an extension of the green plains of South Gujarat while the area of Nagar Haveli is a hilly terrain and is surrounded by the ranges of Sahyadri mountain (Western Ghat). The slopes are generally exceedingly steep. The principal river, the Daman Ganga passes through its hilly terrain and intersects it. It's tributaries are Varna, Pipri and Sakart (or Sakaltal or Sakaltod as some people pronounce it). The Daman Ganga rises in the Ghat-64 Km. from the sea coast and discharged itself in the Arabian Sea at Daman. It is a seasonal river but rises to its brink during monsoon. The central region of the land is almost plain where soil is fertile and rich. The climate is moderate and healthy in the central zone though hot during summer. The area has high humidity and medium temperature. Rainy season is normal from June to September, average rainfall approximately 2000 to 2500 mm. within a period of about 80 days. In central region, the soil is deep and clay and crack during the summer. In the northern and southern portions, the soil tends to be shallow with a considerable portion of 'Murrum' on account of erosion caused by the practice of shifting cultivation. Out of the total area of 48,882 hectares (Census of India 1981-Part III-A & B) Series 27, page - 5) 24,047 hectares are covered by the crops such as paddy, wheat, *ragi* (madua), *jowar, bajra* (millets) and pulses of *tur* and *moong,* oil seeds and sugarcane. Brinjal, tomato, cabage, cauliflower etc. are the main vegetables grown in the territory in the area of a mere 22 hectares. The territory contains no minerals as no proper geological survey has been carried out. Forest is an important natural resource of the territory. Timber trees like *teak, sadra, khair, mahra* and *sisam* constitute the main wealth of the territory. Other timber trees are *lalkhair* (acasica sundra), *tiwas* (dalbergia ougeinersis), siwana (omedina urborea), *dambora* (conocarpus lati falia), *hedu* (nanclea cordifolia), *asana* (brielia spinusa), *temburri* (diaspyros montana) and *babul* (accacia tree). Forest occupies an area of 20,852 hectares which is 43% of the total geographical area. The area of forest is spread over 58 villages. New plantation has been introduced in the forest area, to enrich the forest wealth and also to meet the demand of expensive trade and *khair* wood. The region has provided birds, viz. *lawi* and other forest birds, and animals such as wildcat, *shashla* (rabbit), dear, leopard etc. The people domesticate cattle, buffaloes, sheep, goat and poultries.

Under the treaty of Poona Nagar Haveli was given to Portugese in 1783 as compensation for a vessel destroyed by the Maratha navy, whereas Dadra was ceded to them by a treaty in 1785 as a kind of fief by the local ruler. The socio-economic profile of Dadra and Nagar Haveli (Census of India 1971 page 3) says that about the treaty between the Marathas and the Portuguese, said to have been concluded on 17.12.1779. There are strong doubts about its authenticity as there are at least four drafts and it appears that none was finally concluded. In any case it is curious that even in its Portuguese version, the treaty does not transfer sovereignty over these enclaves from the Marathas to the Portuguese government. It further says that as the Portuguese have acted with the greatest friendship towards the Sarkar as proved by the

Narayen Vithal Dumo, the Sarkar shall give the Daman village for 12,000/- rupees without having any dominion or any other form of hatred on the part of the Sarkar and in which Portuguese shall not erect buildings in accordance with the arrangements made and the village shall be specially mentioned. In 1923, Mr. Maniz published a book entitled '*Noticias a Documetos para a Historia de Damao Antiga Provincia de Norte*' in which he reproduced the treaty concluded at Puneem. The Portuguese plunderers demanded Rs.12000/-from the king of Puneem, for preserving friendship. This sum was given to them in the form of the assignment of 66 villages of Nagar Haveli on 10.6.1783. Not contented with the demand and talking advantage of the declining power of the Maratha king, they demanded an additional number of villages, under the pretext that the income from the villages mentioned before was below Rs.12,000/-. Consequently Marathas handed over the income of another seven villages on 7.7.1785 which included the important village of Dadra, while Goa League (1957, page 8) says that Dadra was occupied on 22.7.1785. Imperial Gazeetteer (1908 vol XI page 296) also says that 72 villages of Dharampur (a Jagir of Maratha) were wrested from the state by the Marathas early in eighteenth century. The territory was liberated step by step i.e. Khanval was liberated on 19.7.54, Dadra on 22.7.54 and the Administrator of the Pargana of Dadra and Nagar Haveli surrendered near Udhwa on 15.8.1954 as per the information received from J.N. Dessai of Lavacha.

The jagir of Nagar Haveli and Dadra were part of the Dharampur state under the dominion of Maratha Peshwas. The State, part of ancient North Konkan, was ruled by Sisodia king of Chittorh. Imperial Gazatteer (1902, Vol. XI-296) also supports this. Gazetteer of Goa, Daman and Diu (1979 Part II & III - page 18) states that the Rajput king Ram Shah, after losing his ancestral patrimony in Udaipur during Muslim conquest, came down to south and seems to have defeated the Koli chief, Nathout, and established himself in the hilly tract of Asheri or Asserseta near Daman about 1262 AD. Parmar says that this part was known as Konkan and ruled by Konkan rulers from ancient times and was also known as Apyantak. The area has also been referred to in Mahabharat when Sahdev won the area during Pandavas Rajsuya yagna. It is believed that from time to time the area was ruled by Kalriyan, Mauryan, Shilahar, Yadavas and Magadha kings and name Konkan has been given after the Kalmyans. It was again ruled by the Solankis from the tenth century to twelfth century. As mentioned earlier, the Sisodia ruler, Ram Singh, after defeating the Koli-chief, established the state of Ram Nagar. His descendants ruled the state till 1472. The part of Sanjan state was conquered by Sultan of Gujarat Muhammad Begda in 1468. The Parsi took asylum under Ramnagar ruler Jagat Shah. He was succeeded by Rana Jaidev in 1531. Portuguese attacked Daman in 1553, defeated the Afghan defender of the Daman fort, and conflict erupted between Portuguese and Jaidev. Having realized the strength of Jaidev the Portuguese made friendship with him after handing over the custody of Daman to the ruler. The name Jaidev was given to Rana Jagat Shah II and since then Maharanas of Ramnagar started suffixing Dev. In 1566, the king was busy with the confrontation with the Portuguese from Thana and Chaulhi and the Sultan from south. He accepted the sovereignty of Mughal King Akbar after meeting Todarmal in Gujarat in 1568. He defeated the Jawars, once a part of Ramnagar, with the help of Portuguese, and expanded his empire. He died in 1600. His son Ramdev ruled from 1600 to 1635 who was succeeded by Somdev with his capital at Atereta. The Maratha ruler Shivaji captured the state in 1644, when he attacked Surat to secure a convenient passage from Thana to Surat. Somdev shifted his capital from Atereta to Nagar Fatehpur, eight miles east of Gambhir Garh, which was the fort of Ramnagar state. Afterwards Shivaji returned the state along with some part of Nasik to Somdev. In 1680 Somdev was succeeded by Maharana Sahadev, who reestablished his capital at Atereta after the death of Shivaji. Shambhuji, son of Shivaji, maintained his alliance with Sahadev. Ramnagar state flourished only under Maharana Sahadev again after Ramdev. The original inhabitants viz. Koli, Varli, Kukna were trained by the ruler as soldiers and farmers. Eventually, Dadra and Nagar Haveli, the part of Ramnagar State, were ceded to portuguese by the Marathas in 1783-85 and remained under Portuguese rule as a Pargana of Daman. Ballal (Census of India 1971, page 7) reports that after, the takeover by the Portuguese, there were for many years, violent disputes with Raja of Dharampur.

The anti-colonial struggle began with the advent of Carles Du Cruz, a Goan, who was appointed a teacher in the Portuguese school of Silvasa in September, 1930. He started publication of a nationalist newspaper 'Sandalcao'. As a consequence of his nationalist activities he was dismissed on 29.9.1932. He continued his support to the Goan Nationalist Movement and had connections with T.B. Cunha, Goan Nationalist leader. Goa League (1957:11) states that while the struggle

1953 to the enclave of Nagar Haveli and Dadra, the weakest parts of the Portuguese 'empire' in India. It further says (page 12) that in August, 1953 the Chief Commissioner of Daman, Mr. Revez Romba, realising that struggle was gaining strength, invited the president of the United Front of Goans and other Goan leaders to discuss a scheme for grant of wide political autonomy to Portuguese leaders. The leaders, on their arrival at Daman, were insulted, illtreated and pressurised to make a declaration which they refused. The excitement spread among the Goan Nationalists and they decided to make a final and determined effort towards the liberation of the enclaves. Ballal (1971-7) further says that in January 1954 intensive nationalist campaigns began in Nagar Haveli. T.B.Cunha, Peter Alvares and A.K Karmakar arranged a public meeting in Vapi which was also attended by J.N. Dessai of Lavacha and the people of Dadra and Nagar Haveli, specially Goman Singh of Naroli and Bam Muli Das Ghela Bhai Bhawsar. From April to May 1954 several public meetings were held on the border of Nagar Haveli, and one such meeting was addressed by Sri Jai Prakash Narain, the Indian Socialist leader on 17.5.54. The Portuguese became alarmed and the Chief Commissioner of Daman sent a confidential order to the Chief of the Police at Silvasa to take prompt action and use force, if necessary, to protect the sovereignty of Portuguese Government. Some of the Goan Nationalists wanted to liberate Dadra peacefully by winning over the police force, others wanted direct action. The United Front of Goans with the aid of Goan Peoples' Party and other nationalists, led by Francis Masceranhas, entered Dadra on 21.7.1954 in the night and after a brief scuffle, Anashet Rusario, the Chief of Dadra Police Chowki, was defeated by the volunteers at 2 a.m. on 22.7.54. Francis Masceranhas was proclaimed the commander of Dadra at 8. A.M. on 22.7.54 and J.N. Dessai as Sarpanch on 26.7.54. Naroli was freed on 28th July by the inhabitants led by Guman Singh, assisted by the revolutionaries. From Dadra the Nationalists marched into Nagar Haveli on 29.7.54 and the panic striken Portuguese force decided to run away and left Silvasa with the Administrator Fidalogo and Chief of Police, and took shelter in the forest near Sialy. The Nationalists reached Silvasa on 2.8.54 and posted about 100 volunteers on 3.8.54. The Administrator's family was brought to Daman. The Portuguese from Sialy crossed the Daman Ganga river and went to Kharoli and then to Khanvel and finally surrendered before Nagarwala, DIG, CID Maharashtra with the Chief of Police Falkaon on 13.8.54 and the whole territory was proclaimed as liberated on the Indian Independence Day, 15.8.54 by Senhor Gama, the oldest man of Nagar Haveli. A.N. Karmakar was made Administrator, Nana Kajrakar, Chief of Police, and T.B. Cunha, president of the Action Committee, hoisted the flag at Silvasa. A nominated panchayat was formed in November 1954 and Narayan G. Chambal was elected as the first Sarpanch of Silvasa and J.N. Dessai as the Sarpanch of Naya Panchayat. The Portuguese accused the Indian Government of their involvement and requested it to allow the Portuguese troops and Police to cross through the Indian territory into the enclave of Dadra. They were not permitted to enter the Indian soil. Indian government replied that it could not be a party to the suppression of genuine nationalist movement for freedom from foreign rule. The Portuguese appealed to the International Court of Justice at the Hague but the court gave the judgement in favour of Indian Governemnt on 12.4.1960. The first elected Administrative-cum-Legislative Council of Dadra and Nagar Haveli unanimously voted on June 13, 1961 for merger with Indian Union. Ballal (Census of India, 1971 page - 11) says that the Goan Action Committee composed of all Goan parties in Bombay used to appoint the Administrator till the Centre took over the Administration. The elected members of Dadra and Nagar Haveli were invited to Delhi on 8.8.1961 and the Bill for the merger was introduced in the Lok Sabha, which received the President's consent and finally Dadra and Nagar Haveli were integrated with the Union of India on 11.8.1961. It was under the Ministry of External Affairs till 31.8.61 and from that date it has been under the control of the Ministry of Home Affairs.

The Union Territory at present comprises 71 villages and one town (Silvassa is declared as Census town as per 1981 Census). The Collector is the head of the Union Territory while the Governor of Goa is the Administrator of the territory. The Dadra and Nagar Haveli Village Panchayat Regulation, 1965 was brought into force with effect from 2.10.65 and the Sarpanch was elected. Panchayat consists of a group of villages with a Group Panchayat. In all, there are ten Group Panchayats which include 72 villages. The Advisory Committee includes the Sarpanch of the Group Panchayats with Collector as the Chairman. In 1989 a Pradesh Council, having two members, was established. Prior to that there used to be a Varishtha Panchayat. The Union Territory has one Parliamentary Reserved Constituency.

Census operation and ethnographic survey from 1806 onwards helped to identify the communities under the People of India project in helped to identify the communities under the People of India project in 1986-89 for the country as a whole. During field operation in the region the recurrence of the names of six communities, out of 23, in Maharashtra, Gujarat, Daman and Diu was reported. Again five communities, out of 23, were reported missing in the Union Territory. They might have either migrated or intermingled with the other communities of the territory. On the other hand, three more communities were identified during the course of field operation. In all fourteen communities were covered in the Union Territory viz. Agri, Bharwad, Chamar, Dhodia, Dubla, Kahar, Kapadia, Kathodi, Kokna, Koli Dhor, Makrana, Mauri Rajput, Parsi and Varli. The study presents detailed write ups on each community of the territory based on empirical anthropological survey in the sixteen villages, which laid the foundation of a comprehensive ethnography of the people of Dadra and Nagar Haveli.

The Union Territory of Dadra and Nagar Haveli was part of the then Dharampur state under the Marathas before it was ceded to the Portuguese. Traditionally, the people follow the life and culture of Gujarat and ancient Konkan region, 40% of which was under forest. About 80% population consists of the tribals who are honest and simple. The economic, social and cultural affinities of the inhabitants are with those of adjacent and contiguous Gujarat and Maharashtra border areas. As a result, both socially and economically, they are in no way different from their brethren of Gujarat and Maharashtra.

The ethnic composition of Dadra and Nagar Haveli comprises Hindus, viz. the Mauri Rajput, Kahar, Kapadia, Agri, Bharwad, Chamar; the colourful tribals viz. Varli, Kokna, Kathodi, Dhodia, Dubla, Koli Dhor; the Parsi, the Khoja, the Makrana and the Catholic Christians. The Varli, Kokna, Koli Dhor are said to be the original inhabitants of the territory before the Sisodias conquered the state. The Mauri Rajput, a section of the Parmars migrated from Abu to Chitorh, from Chitorh to Lata (presently Bharooch) and then to Dharampur State. They were given the Subedari of Dadra and Nagar Haveli by the then king of Dharampur State. Others migrated from various places of Gujarat and Maharashtra. The Parsi took shelter in the territory after the fall of Sanjan (the then neighbouring State) at the hands of the Sultan of Gujarat. The Makranas were brought in by the Sisodia ruler as soldiers and were subsequently deputed under the Subedari of Nagar Haveli. The Kathodi were brought in by the Parsi for their business of liquor and catechu production from Maharashtra. The Christian settled down after Portuguese occupied the territory. Only a few Christian landlords continued to live in their settlements even after the fall of Dadra and Nagar Haveli.

The territory does not have a single settlement in which various communities share a common and compact settlement site. It presents a nucleated settlement around which all the villages are established. The nucleus is in the centre of the territory in Naroli, Silvasa, Dadra and Khanvel, while the scattered settlements, mainly of the tribals in the villages, are in the range of ten to fifteen kilometers on way to the town. The nucleated settlement is inhabited by the Mauri Rajput, Kapadia, Agri, Kahar, Chamar, Bharwad, Khoja and the Christian, while the scattered settlements in the forest area of the hilly terrain, on the east, north- east and south-east border, are inhabited by the Varli, Kokna, Koli Dhor, Kathodi, Dhodia, Dubla and Makrana. The Parsi are the landlords and live in scattered settlements. The Mahar came from Maharashtra during the construction of Daman Ganga Reservoir project and went back after the completion of the project and the Census operation of 1981.

Road is an important means of transportation. The territory a has good network of roads throughout the territory linking all its villages as well as the villages of Gujarat and Maharashtra. Ballal (1971:18) says that till 1966 the territory had 38 miles of roads and 125 miles of cart tracks. The network of the roads consists of 47.6 kms. of black topped, 88.4 kms. of water bound Macedam, 26.4 kms. of other metalled roads 29.6 kms. of other unmetalled roads. Owing to heavy rainfall and absence of bridges at many points, most of the roads are usable only during fair weather. Previously, road transport was operated by private enterprises and there was a great deal of inefficiency. Faquir Chand (1987:5) reports that the total road length in the territory is 325 Kms. Now there are better arrangements of transport made by the Gujarat State Transport Authorities. Facilities of regular bus services are available as far as possible. As Silvasa is situated midway between Bombay and Surat, it is linked by National Highway No. 8. Vapi, the nearest railway station is located between Bombay and Surat and is 15 kms. west of Silvasa. All Group Panchayats and C.D.P. Blocks have sub-post offices. The head post office is at Silvasa. The telephone system which was put into operation by the Free Administration connecting all local offices at Silvasa and ten Group Panchayats/ Patellads (revenue units) of the territory is continuing.

Ecological conditions influence the pattern of the construction of house. They also reflect the economic conditions of the people. The houses of tribals in the villages are erected in the forest and hilly area with thatch, clay, straw, leaves and bamboo available there. The dwellings have roofs of straw, leaves, reeds and bamboo. The floor of the hutments is made of beaten earth covered with cowdung emulsion which is believed to possess antiseptic properties. The well to do families have the walls built with unburnt bricks and stone. The roofs are covered with *deshi* or country tiles. The Parsi have walls built of stone and burnt brick and roof of Manglore tiles, wood and bamboo. The Mauri Rajput, Kapadia, Christian and Agri in the town have pucca houses with stone walls plastered with cement, and roof of Mangalore tiles or cement concrete with two to three storeys - right from the Portuguese period . The tribals in hilly areas have a small rectangular open courtyard in the front, covered with thatched roof. Under its shade they rest and spend their leisure hours. All the houses are a single storeyed structure and have one or two rooms. In case of the availability of only one room, cooking is done in one corner, sleeping in another, and other two corners are used for bathing and storing. In case of two rooms, one room is used as bedroom and the other is used as kitchen and bathroom, where water pots and water storing utensils are also kept. The houses are generally unfurnished. They keep their livestock near their residential areas. Drainage facilities are totally absent. Used water is thrown around the huts. Concepts of cleanliness and sanitation are beyond their perception. Outer verandah is a common feature of houses in the territory. Men and women in the village go for nature call in the field or forest. Houses in town, however, are well built with the provision of bathroom, toilet, bed room, kitchen and drawing room. The drainage system is well maintained. The Parsi living in the village have pucca houses with all modern amenities.

Ornaments reflect the economic condition and taste of the people. For tribals, ornaments serve the purpose of displaying affluence and augmenting beauty. The colourful tribals are very fond of adorning their hairlocks with *pavalakayan* or stringed strands of coin. They wear bangles on their hands and *diyan* over elbow as an armlet. Bangles are made of plastic or glass. *Nath* or *vali* (nose ring) is made of silver. Ear ornaments consists of ear clip and *paganan* (chain) which is attached to ear clips. Married women use *hansli* (collar). Ornaments are made of silver and nickel. These are *sankal* (anklet), *paganan* (chain), *pavalaakyan* (necklace), bangles, armlets, bead necklace, *jhulakiyan* (ear rings), *eliyan* (armlets), *grauthi* (necklace), *mangalsutra, hansali* (collar), *nath* (nose ring), *jodwa, har* (necklace). The tribal women wear all these ornaments during marriage. The Rajputs, Parsi, Kapadia, Agri and Makrana generaly wear the ornaments made of gold. Men put on very few ornaments compared to women. In general only among the tribals, men wear ornaments. They put on silver *kada* (armlet) on wrist and *bandi*. Girls sometimes wear strings of beads of different colours around their necks.

The Varli, Kokna, Kathodi and Koli Dhor generally dress in small loin cloth and a few wear *dhoti* which always remains above knee. Now-a-days the young boys working outside on roads, in offices and industries wear *pyjama* (trousers). Men wear a half sewn tunic called *bandi* resembling a waist cloth over a shirt. The head gear (*fenta*) is wrapped on the head with one end hanging loose and the other tucked over the front. However, some Dhodia and Dubla put on the white cap of *khaddar* (handloom). The *bandi* is usually made of cheap grey cotton cloth called *doti*. Stripped cotton cloth with grandy colours are preferred for the shirt. Women wear *lugda* (saree) made of five to six yards of cheap cotton cloth, dark or red, green or sky blue. The manner of putting on *saree* is peculiar. It is worn with a *kachhota* with the front pleats tucked behind, but instead of loose end or *palav* wrapping the breast around the left shoulder, it is wound up round the waist and tucked at the waist on the right. Their *choli* (blouse) is like a Maharashtrian buttonless blouse, the lower corners of which are tied in the knot above the waist in front to cover the breast. *Odhani* is two to three yards of red, yellow or green colours, and serves the purpose of covering the head. Now tribal women a wear blouse in place of *kachhota*. The men of higher castes wear pant-shirt, *dhoti*, as they do in Gujarat. The Parsi wear *pyjama, kurta* and headgear in black colour. The Christian generally wear the European dress. Young tribal children wear loin cloth while the children from other communities wear bush-shirts and half pants. Small tribal girls wear a blouse and a loin cloth while younger tribal girls wear a blouse and a small *lugda* in the same manner as the women wear.

The tribals of the territory are pre-eminently agriculturists or are involved with allied activities. Their staple food includes the cereals *nagli* (coarse quality of rice), rice and *jowar*, pulses of *tur* and *urad*. They are nonvegetarian who eat fresh as well as dried fish, meat of goat, sheep, deer, *shashla* (rabbit), crab, wild pig and fowls. They also eat vegetables to add flavour to their dishes. Sometimes they, especially the Kathodi and Koli Dhor, also consume roots and tubers. These are *terri, tomon, koduka, jeri, lunda* and tender sprouts of bamboo. Their breakfast includes *rotla* (thick bread) made of *nagli* or rice or *jowar* with salt. For lunch they take rice, or *rotla* of rice or *jowar* with pulses and dry fish. Their dinner consists of *rotla* with vegetables. The Hindu non-tribals are also nonvegetarian, who eat fish, meat of goat, rabbit, deer and fowls especially on the festive occasions. Their staple food includes wheat, rice, *jowar*, pulses of *tur* and *urad* and locally available seasonal vegetables. The Christian, Makrana and Parsi have similar food habits. Tribals are very fond of drinking *daru* (home made liquor) and toddy. Alcoholic drinks are enjoyed by all communities except the Makrana. Smoking is common to all but the tribals make their own *bidi* with tobacco and *sanghai* or *timroo* leaves whenever they have a desire for smoking. The non-tribals smoke *bidi* as well as cigarettes purchased from market. *Shovele, kitchri* and *kanji* (gruel) of *jowar* or *nagli*, which is prepared after grinding and boiling *jowar* or *nagli* in water,are enjoyed on festive occasions by the tribals. *Puri* (fried bread), *srikhand* (made of sugar and curd), *dudh pak* (rice boiled in milk with sugar) and *dhokla* are the special food preparations. The Christians and Makranas prepare *biriyani* (fried rice with mutton), *zarda* and non- vegetarian dishes on the festive occasions. The non-tribals also consume seasonal fruits. Ground nut oil is used as cooking medium by all the communities.

The tribals have their cots made of bamboo sticks. They have fishing nets, bows and arrows and bird traps. They also use baskets of different sizes, *ghanti* (hand grinder), *khunti* (hanger made of *kirmira* tree), *day* (wooden spoon), *malai* and *wang* (fishing hooks), rope of the bark of *dhamy* tree, *supado* (winnowing fan), *shavree* (broom), *tavi* (hot plate) and *tapali* (ovan). The tribals use earthen and alluminium utensils while among the non tribals, Muslims, Parsi and the Christians, the utensils are of brass and steel. Music is played on social as well as on religious occasions. Dancing is part of their life. Their musical instruments include both wind and percussion instruments such as *torpa* (made of pumpkin), *chang* (bamboo flute), *tur*, brass *thali, kahli, dhol* (drum made of sagwan wood and goat skin), *kadi* (drum beater), *pawi* (flute), *ghangli* (pyjab) and *timki* (a small drum leathered on only one side). The non-tribals engage the tribals as musicians while the

Rajputs, Kapadia, Makrana and Christian bring modern musicians from various places in marriages. During festivals like Holi, the tribals are invited as musicians. The agricultural tools used by them are generally indigenous, mainly made by themselves with wood. The largely used agricultural implements are *hal* (plough), *karal/karab* (harrow), *samar* (toothed harrow) and *vavnio*. Different types of iron axes and spades namely *datedy* (sickle), *kodala* (hoe), *kad*, *kuhadi* (axe) and *pavdo* (shovel) are supplements to these implements. The craft of basketry and leather works are some other cultural elements. The craft of basketry is mainly found among the Koli Dhor and Varli who make *ghanghari* (rain coat), *torpa* (musical instrument of bamboo), *pati* (basket of bamboo leaves), *sunppa* (winnowing fan), *tokra* (basket) and *tatki* (mat). These products are made of bamboo and teak wood leaves. The craft of leather is practised by the Chamar who purchase the raw materials from the Koli Dhor.

There are many tribal art forms viz. graphic arts, wall paintings, tattooing, music, folk songs and folk dances. The Varli wall paintings, floor designs are quite famous. The tribals are fond of *godhely/tarjwana* (tattooing). Various signs are tattooed on chin, below lower lip, on forehead, on cheeks, on nose and on feet. They get themselves tattooed by the tattooer in the weekly markets between the age of five to fifteen years. The various folk songs are sung by men as well as women during birth, betrothal, marriage, pregenancy and delivery, religious rituals, and also during plantation of seed and harvesting. Both tribal and non-tribal folk dances are performed in the territory. The tribal folk dances include *bhowada* (mask made of *pangara* and *samar* wood) in summer, *torpa* (after plantation of paddy), *dhol* performed only by the Kokna men and *tur thali* by the Dhodia and Dubla. *Garba* and *dandiaras* are the other forms of folk dances common among the Hindu communities. These dances are preformed only by women.

The main festivals observed by the Varli, Kokna, Kathodi and Koli Dhor are Shun Barash and Bhawada. Diwasa is the main festival of the Dhodia and Dubla. They also celebrate other non-tribal festivals such as Holi, Diwali and Akha Teej. Hindu celebrate Navratri, Atham, Nag Panchami, Holi, Shivaratri and Rakshabandhan. The Makrana celeberate Id-ul-Fitar, Id-ul-Zoha and Muharram. Holi is main fair of the tribals held at Lavacha, a village in Gujarat, situated between Tighra and Amli villages of the territory. Non-tribals are also participants. Shivratri fair is the major fair of the Hindus.

Dhodia and Dubla. The dialect spoken by the various tribals within the community members are Dhodi by the Dhodia, Dubli by the Dubla, Kathodi by the Kathodi, Kokni by the Kokna and Koli Dhor, Varli and Dabar by the Varli with the influence of Gujarati and Marathi and Chamri by the Chamar. The Makrana speak Makrani which is similar to Baluchi. The Christian speak Portuguese. The major scripts used are Gujarati, Roman, Devnagari and Arabi. The non-tribals are also conversant with Hindi and English.

The total population of the territory was 24,280 in the year 1900 which increased to 57,963 in the Census carried out after liberation in 1962. According to Census of India, 1981 (page X III A & B, Series - 27, 1983) the total population of the territory is 1,03,676 out of which 52,515 are males and 51,161 are females. Out of the total population 2041 i.e. 1.97% are the scheduled castes and 81,714 i.e. 78.82% are the scheduled tribes. They were scheduled under the Article 341 (1) and 342 (2) of the Constitution of India in 1962. There has been decrease in the tribal population during 1961 to 1981. It was 88.5% at the time of 1961 Census, 86.89% at the time of 1971 Census and 78.82% at the time of 1981 Census. Decrease in population might have been due to their migration to the bound areas of Gujarat and Maharashtra, because of their involvement in various industries. About 1932 are Muslim, 2025 are Christian and other communities are 19,921. According to 1981 Census the total population of the Parsi is only 26. The population of Dadra and Nagar Haveli in 1981 which was 103,676 increased to 138,477 in 1991 showing a 33.57 percent growth rate during the decade 1981-91.

Table Showing Decadewise Variation in the population of Dadra and Nagar Haveli, 1900-81

Year	Total population	Variation	Males	Females
1900	24,280	-	12,386	11,894
1910	29,020	19.50%	14,754	14,266
1921	31,048	6.9 %	16,008	15,040
1931	38,260	23.23%	20,017	18,243
1940	40,441	5.70%	21,009	19,432
1950	41,532	2.70%	27,345	20,187
1962	57,963	39.56%	29,524	28,439
1971	74,170	27.96%	39,964	37,206
1981	103,676	39.78%	52,515	51,161

Ref: Census of India 81, Part - III Series - 27, Dadra and Nagar Haveli, Directorate of Census Operation Panaji, 1988, page-150.

The religious beliefs and practices of various communities of the territory are shaped by the major religions such as the religion practised by the tribals, Hinduism by the Hindu, Islam by the Makrana, Christianity by the Christians and tribal Christian converts, and Zoroastrianism by the Parsi. The tribals worship deities associated with the totemic objects and spiritual power. Gam Dev and Wagh Dev (tiger God) are the main deities. Hirwa Dev, Pitar Nirbhanjhi, Khardra, Chitoba Mair and Himan Devi are their clan deities. There are other deities also viz. Kansari Devi (deity of grain) and Makar Devi (deity of harvesting). Considering food as life giver, the tribals have highest reverence for corn as deity. As they are inhabitants of forest, Wagh Dev is considered to be the main deity who protects them and their cattle in village from the wild beasts. The particular deity is worshipped ceremoniously once in a year on *Krishna Paksha Dwadashi* (twelfth day of dark half) of Ashwin month when *sindur* (vermillion) is applied and a goat is sacrificed. *Bhagat* performs the ritual. This status is next to the Patil (head). He also officiates at their life cycle rituals whose exorcises the evil spirits during the illnesses. The younger ones are initiated into *bhagatship* at an isolated place on some hill or in *raval* initiated into *bhagatship* at an isolated place on some hill or in *raval* (training place) where they learn the art of inducing fits or deliriums which qualify them to act as a medium between God and common man. Girha is the spirit of water. Cheda and Hadli are male and female spirits which are propitiated by the *bhagat*. The tribals also have faith in some of the Hindu deities viz. Hanuman, Laxmi and Shiva.

The major deities of the Hindu are Ganapati, Shiva, Hanuman and Ambamata. Apart from these, they have also their *kul* (family or clan) deities. Sword is an important object of the Rajput which is worshipped during the life-cycle rituals. Brahman officiates at the life cycle rituals of the Hindu except the Chamar who employ *bhagat* of Varli or Kokna to conduct the rituals of marriage and sorcery. The main object of worship for Parsi is Holi Fire which is placed at *agyari* (temple at Udhwada in Gujarat). Christianity had a great impact on the tribals who were converted after the Portuguese occupied the area. Though in the treaty of 1779 it was stipulated that Portuguese would not attempt conversions in the Maratha dominated empire, after gaining control over the tribal dominated territory, they started converting the tribals forcibly, especially the young children who never knew when they were baptised. According to Bhatia (1986, page 16), association of the individuals with the church was given tremendous publicity. Hostel admission, free education as well as food were provided to converts or to those who were on the way of conversion. Teaching and other jobs in the mission were used as other allurments. Bhatia further (page 18) says that casual sojourn to the interior villages of Kauncha, Beldari, Bedpa, Khedpa, Dapada, Mandoni, Sinduri, Sheli, Khanvel reveals that tribal households, have Christian images set up in their homes, worship the cross, have Christian names and attend feasts and functions organised by the mission, although they have retained Hindu names in the Census roll.

Apart from the five major religions, other sects are also flourishing among the Hindu communities. There are followers of Jalaram sect, a saint and devotee of Lord Rama, Krishanities, Shirdi Ke Sain Baba, Jai Guru Dev sect, initiated by Sri Mukta nand Swami in Maharashtra, Shanti Panth, Gayatri Pariwar, and Swami Narayan.

The economy of Dadra and Nagar Haveli revolves around agriculture and forest. The Varli and Kokna communities living in forest are now the cultivating tribes. Till late sixties they used to practise slash-and-burn cultivation but due to the Government policy to check deforestation they have taken up terrace and settled cultivation. The agricultural produce includes *nagli*, rice, *jowar*. They have to depend mainly on rain water. They also work as agricultural labour and forest labour. Besides, they produce honey and charcoal from the forest. The Kathodi were brought in by the Parsi from Maharashtra for making liquor and catechu. They were given loans, and thus became bonded to the landowners. The Koli Dhor are skin hiders and agricultural labours. They provide skin of the dead animals to the Chamar for leather craft. The Mauri Rajput, Kapadia, Agri, Dhodia, Parsi and Dubla communities, whose occupation was cultivation, established rapport with outsiders for the purpose of producing and exchanging commodities. They produce cereals and millets such as wheat, paddy, *bajra*, *jowar*, *ragi*; pulses like *tur*, *moong* and *urad*, and the cash crops such as sugarcane, tobacco, raw cotton, mustard seeds and ground nut. They also practise horticulture and grow banana, mango, *chiku*, coconut, etc. They sell off their products in the markets of Silvasa, Vapi and Valsad. The Kahar are the only community engaged in selling of dry fish. Animal husbandry, industrial labour, transport and some other trades are the other means of livelihood for communities. They are also merchants, contractors and casual labours; or are in service.

The development process has brought about many changes in the economy of the people specially of the tribals, after liberation. The new set-up of the Administration of Dadra and Nagar Haveli, with a view to improving the economy of the people, took measures such as introduction of Land Reforms Regulation 1971, which became effective on 1.5.74. Lands were distributed to the landless tribals. 1787.62.95 hectares of land were distributed in 1985. Loan-cum-subsidy of 50% has been introduced to help the tribal and scheduled caste in agriculture, animal husbandry and horticulture. The Act of Gujarat Cooperative Societies 1964, was also introduced in the territory in 1982 under the schemes of Large Size Multi Purpose Cooperative Society and Primary Agricultural Credit Society. The Community Development Programmes were induced through the Blocks in April, 1963. When the rains are not adequate, the Administration tries to provide the jobs to the tribals through construction of roads and in forests. Efforts are made to safeguard the interests of the tribals and the land mortgaged to the non-tribals was also given back to the tribals by the Administration. The industrial complex at Pipariya near Silvasa has provided the job opportunities to the tribals. The Kathodis, who earlier worked under the Parsi as bonded labour, were freed in 1985-86, and have now been provided land and houses under Indira Awas Yojna. The tribals also get chemical fertilizer through agricultural societies on 50% loan- cum-subsidy basis. The free education for tribals and opening of more educational institutions have provided the job opportunities to the tribals as well as to the non-tribals.

From early youth the people are exposed to the myth and traditions and though they receive little education of a formal nature, they learn as they grow up, first in the family and later in the bigger circle of the villagers to imbibe the social values and ethics that govern the life of the people. The level and mechanism of social control of the various communities are regulated by their traditional caste councils which are referred to as *samaj* among the tribals, *panch* among the Rajput, *jamat* among the Makrana and *anjuman* among the Parsi. They are headed by a Patil or Pramukh who are elected by voice vote. They are assisted by a *karbhari* (care taker) from each *parha* (hamlet). Only the Koli Dhor have their Patil as tribal head which is a heriditory post. The traditional councils regulate the daily activities within the village, on regional and inter-regional level. The chief function of these councils is to bring-toegther the members of the community, to punish the miscreants, to prevent breach of customary laws and to adjudicate in civil and other matters which may upset the equilibrium of the communities. They also take decisions in economic and religious matters and inter-community disputes. Even minor criminal assaults are resolved by the tribal councils at their own level. Excommunication, community feast and cash fine are the forms of punishments imposed by various traditional councils.

With the end of the Portuguese rule and introduction of adult franchise and Panchayat Raj system, a modern political system has emerged. The adult franchise has generated divided feelings among the people and is not considered to be conducive to community unity. The periodical elections for Panchayat, Municipality and Parliamentary constituency have divided the people into factions. One of the major changes in the political set up of the territory is the introduction of Varista Panchayat and Group Panchayat under Panchayati Raj which seeks to provide welfare and implement development programmes.

In every society an individual belongs to a number of groups overlapping in membership and differentiated by functions. All the communities of Dadra and Nagar Haveli enjoy monopoly over an occupation. The system makes people united as well as divided into certain categories. Unity in the sense that they co-operate with each other and are inter-dependent providing assistance in all walks of life. They are divided in the sense that there is stratification among them as they consider themselves superior or inferior to the other in regional social hierarchy. The Mauri Rajputs are considered superior to all in the hierarchy followed by the Kapadia, Agri, Bharwad, Parsi, Dhodia, Kahar, Dubla, Varli, Kokna, Makrana, Chamar, Kathodi and Koli Dhor.

The rule of residence is patrilocal except among some of tribals who practise *khandaria* (marriage by service) and the norm of matrilocal residence. Extended family and nuclear family are common. Its members can be expelled after giving them due share or a member can leave voluntarily. Unmarried woman and other members of the family who possess their own property nevertheless have right to live in the family and the family has an obligation to feed them. Father is the head of the family. The tribals are independent by nature. The houses are so small that the sons, after marriage, generally build their separate houses. The debt incurred, on account of marriage is borne by the new family. The youngest son inherits the residential land. The head of the family is competent to make all acts and contracts. They still abide by the Code of Usages and Custom of Non-Christian Act of 1854 under which the eldest person in the family is empowered to administer all properties, rites and rituals. The income from the self-acquired property can be administered or alienated separately as private property. When a person living in the extended family dies instantly without leaving any descendant and ascendant, the extended family inherits all the property of deceased. A widow succeeds her husband in preference to all other relatives who live separately, including the son. Any person is free to make will in accordance with the General Law (Civil Code of 1887).

Marriage of a boy and a girl belonging to the same *kurh/kul* (clan) usually does not take place and such marriages are considered unlawful according to social customs. The rules of exogamy among the non-tribals are applied upto certain degrees which vary according to the customs prevalent in various communities. This has been discussed separately under communities. The tribals practise cross-cousin marriages. Adult marriage takes place instead of child marriage. Among tribals the mates are acquired through negotiation, *khandaria* (marriage by-service) and mutual consent, whereas the non-tribals negotiate marriage. Both *dej* (dowry) and *pend* (bride price) in cash and kind are in existance among various communities, while *mehar* is in practice among the Makrana. Though polygyny is allowed, they generally practise monogamy. *Natra* (remarriage) or *pat* (widow re-marriage) prevail's among the communities other than the Rajputs.

The life cycle rituals among the Muslim and Christian of territory are governed by the Christian and Islamic laws. Hindu rituals which are common have been discussed under some of the communities. The tribals have set customs for every occasion. These customs have been observed for many years and are considered as good as the laws.

Among the tribals a woman has to observe certain taboos during her pregnancy to ward off evil spirit. Tribals do not have any pre-birth ritual, elderly female members attend to the job of delivery with the help of *suin* (locally trained mid wife from the community). *Pansuthi* is the first post-birth ritual performed on the fifth day after birth when both the child and mother are given bath and the child is ceremonially placed in the *jholi* (cradle) and thus both are free from pollution. *Kurh* (clan) deities are worshipped on sixth day and mother herself names the child. Among the Christian tribal converts, children are named by the Father of the Church. *Babri* (tonsure) of male child is performed after the completion of one year by the maternal uncle. A girl, after her puberty and menstruation, is called *banni*. She is confined for three to four days and cannot enter the kitchen and sacred places. However, she is allowed to carry on working on farms or collecting forest produces or other labour works after four days. She is supposed to wash her hair to become free from pollution. Premarital sex is common among the tribals and such cases are not taken seriously, However, if a girl conceives, the boy is forced to marry her.

Ram-Ram (negotiations) for marriage is initiated by the boy's side. *Bol-dhan* (betrothal) takes place one year prior to marriage. Marriage is performed at the bride's residence. In case of the Kokna, traditionally, the marriage used to be solemnized at the groom's residence, but now there are no firm rules. The venue for marriage is often decided according to the economic conditions of the parties. Marriage rituals are performed for three days and begin with the erection of *mandva* (marriage booth) on first day, followed by *harad* (rubbing of turmeric on the bodies of the both) and worship of *kurh* deity on second day. The groom with the *barhadi* (marriage procession) arrives in the bride's village on the third day. Both the bride and the groom are taken to *mandva* where they make five rounds of the *umar* tree stick (erected in the *mandva*) to perform *fera* (circumambulation) in the midst of the verses recited by the *bhagat* (magico-religious specialist). Tieing of *ganthi* (chain of beads) round the neck of the bride by the groom is the main ritual. Brothers of both the sides lift the couple on their shoulders and thus the rituals are concluded. The groom, with his bride, returns to his village next day after marriage where marriage is consummated. Among the Dhodia and Dubla, *hastmilap, barmal, kanyadan* and tying of *ganthi* are the principal rituals performed in the *chauri* (celestial fire in *mandva*). These are common to all the Hindus. The bride is called back to her parent's house after five days. After five to ten days, the groom with his parents visits the bride's village and brings her back.

Traditionally, the Koli Dhor used to bury their dead. Now all the tribals, except the Christian converts, cremate their dead. Ashes and bones are collected and disposed off in water. *Daru* (liquor) is served after cremation to the funeral party members on their return. *Darhoo* is performed after one month by the *bhagat* to remove pollution. *Kurh* members are invited and liquor is served. *Cheda* (stone memorial) is erected near the crematorium in the name of the deceased. They throw boiled rice on the roof of their houses every year on Diwali in the name of the departed soul.

Among the Parsi, *suin* (tribal trained midwife) is called to attend to the delivery. *Chhathi* is performed on the sixth day after birth. The parents procure the *rashi* name (zodiac name) after examining the stars and planets. The child is named by the parents on the sixth day. They observe birth pollution for 40 days. *Mahino ugadiyo* is performed after one month and after 40 days, *babri* (tonsure) of male child is performed by any lady. *Kusthee* and *shudre* or *navjyot* ceremonies are performed at the age of seven to nine years during which period the sacred thread is tied on the child's body by the *mobid* (priest). *Kusthi* is prepared of 72 threads and *shudre* is of cotton shirt with half sleeves. *Kusthi* is tied over the *shudre* at the waist of the boy.

Bithi chandla (betrothal) takes place after one month to one year prior to marriage at the bride's house. White dress is made for the bride for marriage ceremony. The bridegroom wears coat, pant and black cap and bride wears white *saree* and blouse. Marriage is solemnised at the bride's residence. After the arrival of the bride groom at the bride's residence, both sit on the chairs facing the gathering. *Dasturs* (priests) from both the sides officiate the marriage. Parents of both the sides apply *tilla* (dot) on the forehead with the paste of *kanku*. *Hast milap* (joining of hands) is performed by the priest and *awastha* (their holy verses in Pasand language) and *ashirwad* (blessings in Sanskrit) are recited by the priest while sprinkling rice over the bride and the groom and the couple receive pomegranate as blessings. The bride's father presents *sambha* (dowry) which includes clothing and cash as per economic status. Marriage feast is given by the bride's father. The couple returns to groom's village after some rituals according to Hindu customs are performed.

The Parsi way of disposal of the dead is known. Dead body is exposed at a particular place called *dakhma* (tower of silence). They take the dead body to Nargal in Maharashtra for disposal as there is no *dakhma* in the territory. The dead body is given bath and is covered with white clothes. The clothes are taken off from the body and donated in charity before disposal. *Khandliya* carry the dead to the *dakhama*. They observe death pollution for three days. On fourth day, *chautha* is performed and a feast is given. The mourning period extends for eighteen days and *mukhtad* is performed by the *mobid* (priest) and feast is given.

According to Census of India 1981 (Part XI of A & B Series - 27) in the pre-liberation days there were no industries worth mentioning in the territory. It was only in 1965 that an industrial estate at Silvasa was established. The government of India declared the territory as an industrially backward area so that special incentive could be offered to entrepreneurs for setting up industries. As a result since 1980, there have been about 115 industrial units functioning in the industrial estate. Besides, about 45 small scale units of engineering goods, wire drawing, spun pipe, crimpling of nylon and polyster yarn, plastic moulded articles, chemical and silk fabrics, electrical switches and accessories, detergent powder, dying and printing etc. are in operation. This has provided employment to about 2000 workers. All these developments have taken place after the liberation of the territory from the Portuguese rule. The data, collected in the field, suggest the awareness about the provision of education, health and medical facilities, drinking water and so on.

The installation of a Television Relay Centre at Silvasa is the latest development in the Union Territory. The microwave station was installed in July, 1987. Silvasa is now connected by STD through microwaval link with other parts of the country. Census of India, 1981

(1988:10) states that the implementation of various economic development activities and expansion of government machinery attracted the people of neighbouring states of Gujarat and Maharashtra in search of jobs. With the increase of industrial activities, particularly in the last decade, the Union Territory has witnessed a boost in trade, business and construction activities, giving impetus to economic growth. It (1988:21) further says that during the Portuguese regime agriculture played a prime role in the economy. However, after liberation, the persuits other than agriculture such as service, trade and commerce and industry started gaining importance steadily. Until 1971, more than 50% of its total workers were engaged in the activities related to agriculture. But during the last decade various developmental activities have changed the structure of economy from purely agricultural to service-cum agriculture oriented economy. According to Ballal (1971 Census, Series 1, India No. 10 of 1961 series, page 25) in1963 Community Development Programmes were induced in the territory for the development and upliftment of the weaker sections, specially of the tribals.

Census of India in 1971, generated data on demographic, socio-economic, linguistic and religious parameters. Some publications such as those of Antonio Francisco (1904), Imperial Gazetteer of India (1908), Census of India (1971-81), Bhatia (1986) and Faquir Chand (1987-88) provide scanty ethnographic information on Dadra and Nagar Haveli. A major work in the form of a village study and socio-economic profile of Dadra and Nagar Haveli was done by Ballal (1966-74). Another work on the study of Dapada village is by the Director of Census Operation (1988)). The present study is the first descriptive ethnography of all communities of Dadra and Nagar Haveli in accordance with the paramaters of a modern anthropological study.

N.K. Sinha

AGRI

The Agri are an agricultural community of the Territory. According to Kale (1952 : 1) the name Agri has been derived from the Marathi word 'Agar' which denotes plantation worker of palm tree or a salt pan. Sherring (1974 : Vol. II - 188) contends that the Agri are a division of Kunbi and sub-group of Koli. Enthoven (1920 : Vol. II) noted that the Khatri or Kshatriya descents were transported from Ungri Paithan in the Deccan to Konkan by Bimbaraja after the Deccan was conquered by the Musalman invaders. Kale (1952 : 2), supporting Enthoven's statement states that the soldiers of king Raja Bimba of Sagargadh were provided land for their dwelling and the descendants of these people came to be known as Agris who took to the occupation of agriculture and salt production. According to another legend they migrated from Agra during the period of Moghuls and took asylum in the then Maratha state and finally came and settled in the territory before the advent of Portuguesee.

They perceive their distribution in the villages of Amli and Vaghchipa. They also inhabit Thana and Nasik districts of Maharashtra. Marathi is their language with Devanagari script within the community. They also use Gujarati and Hindi in their dealings with others. They are non-vegetarian who take fish, meat of goat and fowls. Their staple food is rice, *ragi*, pulses of *tur* and *moong*. They also consume locally available fruits and vegetables. Only men take home made alcoholic drinks prepared of *mahurha* and *gurh*. They use ground nut oil as their cooking medium. *Bhajya* (pakoda), *puri* (fried bread), *kachwar*, *kasi* and *dudh-pag* are their special food preparations for Diwali and other festive occasions. They smoke *bidi* and cigarettes.

The Agris are divided into ten exogamous divisions based on *got* (clan). The traceable *gots* are Panwar, Joshi, Mali, Kamde, Bhope, Bhoire, Dangee and Garod. Though Enthoven and Kale have discussed the endogamous division of the Agri, the community does not have any concept of endogamous division. They suffix their *got* to names. The basis of differentiation is social. Main function of *got* is to trace their descent and to regulate their marriage alliances. They perceive their position as inferior to the Brahman, Rajput, Kapadia and superior to the Kahar, Bharwad, Dhodia, Kokna, Dubla, Varli, Parsi, Makrana, Chamar, Koli Dhor and Kathodi in social hierarchy. They are aware of the varna system and recognise their place as Vaishya.

They marry within the community and prefer to marry within the village. The Agri of Maharashtra marry within *tappa* (social limit of marrriage comprising 15 to 50 villages). The rule of exogamy is applied at *got* level and to the extent that a marriage cannot take place within the three ascending generations from the mother's side. Traditionally they practised child marriage. Now they practise adult marriage. The age of marriage for a boy is from 20 to 22 years and for a girl from 18 to 20 years. Marriage is fixed by negotiation only. Though tradition allows them to go for polygyny they practise monogamy. Premarital sex is not allowed. A man can marry his wife's sister after the death of his wife or even in her lifetime if she gives her consent. A married woman ties *kali-ganthi* (marriage pendent) around her neck as her marriage symbol. There is no practice of dowry or bride price. The practice of *kanyadan* exists during marriage. A girl after marriage, goes to stay with her in-laws. *Ṡorchhiti* or *fargati* (divorce) is granted to both men and women by the traditional caste-council. The reasons for divorce are adultery, no male issue, cruelty and misconduct of wife. No *kali ganthi* is broken in divorce. Post-divorce maintenance is the responsibility of her parents. Divorce compensation is given to the aggrieved party. If a divorced woman does not remarry, children get the share in their father's property. They allow *natra* (remarrriage) of widow, widower and divorcee. In case of widow marriage they have to follow the rule of deceased husband's *got* exogamy. A simple ceremony is performed in the night at the house of the widow where only other widows are allowed to participate. Clothes of both the man and woman are knotted together and the Brahman recites the *mantras*. If a widower is marrying an unmarried girl, the regular form of marriage is resorted to in full. The significant change in the marriage rules of the Agri is non-existence of *dej* (dowry) and adult marriage.

Their institution of family consists of extended and nuclear types. The prescribed kinship usages viz. avoidance and joking relationship are maintained within the family members and these practices are common to all the Hindu and tribal communities. Conflict and confrontations in property matters in the family arise after father's death and son's marriage. Rules of inheritance are governed by the Right of Property Act of the Portuguese. But the residential land is inherited by the youngest son who stays with his parents. Eldest son succeeds the authority. Sister's husband play the role of *anwar* (accompanier) and mother's brother brings *maushala* (customary marriage gift) for marriage. Inter-family linkages are stressed during the life cycle rituals, economic activities and during the election of Patel (chief) of the traditional council. Women have low status. They have roles in agriculture, animal husbandry, collection of fuel, bringing potable water, social functions and ritual performances. They also contribute to family income by doing labour. *Fui* (father's sister) has an important role to play during *srimant* (guarding, a pre-birth ritual), *barse* (naming) and *babri* (tonsure) ceremonies.

The life cycle rituals of the Agri are common to all the other Hindu communities of the Territory. *Babri* (tonsure) is performed on male child only. Birth pollution is observed for eleven days. Marriage has become now a one day affair in place of three days. Marriage is solemnized at the bride's residence. *Behwah* (betrothal) takes place one month prior to marriage at the groom's residence. Marriage is consummated at the groom's residence. Death pollution is observed for ten days.

Land is their major economic resource. The community has a mix of both the landowning based on individual proprietorship and the landless. Agriculture is their traditional as well as present primary occupation. Among the people agricultural activities, such as producing crops, are almost on subsistence level. The agricultural implements possessed by them are indigenous. They are mainly dependent on rain water. The crop calender is divided into three parts namely *siara* (winter) for *tur* and *moong*, *unadu* (summer) for *ragi*, *rice* and for *chaumasa* (rainy season) *jowar*. They also work as agricultural labour, casual labour and labourer in industry and in government service. They also produce seasonal vegetables which they sell in daily markets for cash. Crop sharing is also prevalant among them which is locally termed as *bhagidari*. The cultivator's share varies from 40% to 60% but the landowner has to bear the cost of seeds and fertilizers. Agricultural labour receive their wages in cash. The establishment of textile industries at Pipalia and Machhad near Silvasa have provided them opportunities of employment as industrial labour.

Social control is regulated by their *gnyat panch*, the traditional council at village level headed by Patel. Patel is elected by voice vote and is assisted by a *khazanchi* (assistant) and four *sabhya* (members). The tenure of Patel is for three years. Social problems pertaining to adultery, divorce, remarriage are dealt with by the Patel. Pre-marital sex is considered the biggest offence and in such cases the offender is excommunicated. For adultery, the offender is penalised. He must host a feast. Implementing various plans and undertaking development activities are the responsibility of modern statutory *panchayat*.

The Agri profess Hinduism and are the followers of Sanatan Dharm sect. They believe in all the main Hindu deities but their favourite deity is Lord Shiva who is also their villlage god. Hira Mata, Kande Mata are their *got* deities who are worshipped ceremonially on the *athem* (eighth) day of *Magh* month. They also worship Lord Ganesh and Vishnu. Brahman conducts sacred activities. They consider Haridwar, Allahabad, Mathura and Ganesh temple at Bombay as their major shrines. Shivratri is their major fair held at Lord Shiva's temple at Palsana in Gujarat. Their major festivals include Mahaathem, Janmashtami, Bhai Beej, Shivratri and Diwali. They are active followers of Sanatan Dharm movement initiated by Shri Muktanand of Ganeshpuri at Bombay. The community does not have the tradition of art and culture of its own. *Satiyo* (floor design), *tarjana* (tattooing) and *garba* (folk dance) are common to all other Hindu communities.

They accept water and *pucca* or *kachha* food from the Brahman, Rajput and Kapadia, but not from the Kahar, Bharwad, Chamar, Parsi, Makrana and the tribals. They share temple and crematorium with the Kapadia. They also share water resources with others except the Chamar, Varli, Kokna, Dhodia, Dubla, Kathodi and Koli Dhor. They maintain their traditional linkages with the Rajput, Parsi, Dhodia and Dubla with regard to the cultivator and labour relationship and with the Brahman at religious level. They do crop sharing with the Rajput and Parsi. They participate in the Shivratri fair at Palsana with others. The periodical elections have provided them with the chances of interaction with other communities and their political leadership has emerged at panchayat level where they have representation in statutory panchayat. Some of the community members are involved in teaching in addition to some other white collar jobs.

Their attitude towards development programme is positive. The literacy level has gone up where boys study upto college level and drop out from study as they have to earn to support their family. Girls study upto secondary level and drop out from studies due to social reasons and because they have to earn to support their family members. They make use of both the indigenous and modern medicare. Though they favour family planning, they still prefer to have four children. Facilities of piped drinking water, employment in agriculture and confectionary shops and ration distribution are available. Mid-day meal for children and mother-infant care are available under Integrated Child Development Scheme. They make use of electricity, organic manure and chemical fertilisers. Fire wood, cowdung cakes and kerosene oil are their fuel resources. They are exposed to radio, television, cinema, etc.

N.K. Sinha

REFERENCES

Enthoven, R.E, *Tribes and Castes of Bombay*, Vol. I: 1920, Vol. III, 1922, Bombay, The Government Central Press, Reprint, Vol. I & III, pp. 10, 1975, Cosmo Publications, Delhi.

Kale, D.N., *Agri: A Socio-economic Survey*, Asia Publishing House, Bombay, 1952.

Sherring, M.A., *Hindu Tribes and Castes*, Vol. II, 1879, Calcutta, Thakar Spink & Co., Reprint, Vol II., p. 188, 1974, Cosmo Publications, Delhi.

BHARWAD

The Bharwad, a community of herdsmen, are also called Ahir and Dhudhiya Bharwad. Sherring (1976 : Vol. I - 277) has considered them synonymous with the Rabari. Enthoven (1920: Vol. I - 118) and Campbell (1988 Vol. II - 267) regard them as synonymous with the Gaderia, and state that the Bharwad belonged to the caste of Nand Mehar, the foster father of Lord Krishna whose original home was Gokul. This caste is said to have migrated from Gokul to Mewar and then to Kathiawad, then from Kathiawad region of Gujarat to Dharampur state and finally to Silvasa after Portuguese established their rule. The Khasa Ahir was the first to migrate from Chikhali village of Valssad then to Eklash in Umbergaon taluka of Gujarat and finally to Samarvani about 150 years back. They are distributed in the villages of Samarvani, Athal and Naroli of Dadra and Nagar Haveli. Somehow, they are also spread in Saurashtra region of Gujarat. Their spoken language is Kathiawadi and they use Gujarati script for writing. They are also conversant with Hindi. The dress of the women is similar to that of the Rabaris of Kathiawad having resemblance to Rajasthan because of the use of ivory bangles. They wear a *ghagra* (petticoat), a *kapad* (bodice) open behind with loose fitting in front and carried down within an inch or two of the waist of the *ghaghra*.

They are non-vegetarian who eat fish and meat of goat and sheep. Their staple food includes rice, *ragi*, pulses of *tur* and *moong*. They use groundnut oil for cooking. Only men take alcoholic drinks which is a recent change. Traditionally they are fond of taking milk and butter-milk regularly. They take locally available seasonal vegetables and fruits. *Puri* (fried bread), *dhokla* and *lapsee* are the special food preparations made on the festive occasions.

The Bharwad are divided into twenty exogamous divisions based on *kul* or *gotar* (clan) and out of these divisions Chanderka, Roparka, Bamania and Taheka are found in the territory. Enthoven (1920 : Vol.

I - 120) has mentioned 46 surnames. Bamania is considered highest in the social hierarchy. The basis of differentiation is social. The main function of *gotar* is to regulate marriage alliances and trace descent. They suffix Ahir to their names. They perceive their status as inferior to the Brahman, Mauri Rajput, Kapadia, Bania and the Agri in social hierarchy and superior to the Kahar, Chamar, Parsi, Makrana, Varli, Kokna, Koli Dhor, Kathodi, Dhodia and Dubla. They do not recognize varna system.

They marry within the community. The rule of exogamy is applied to *gotar* level and marriage can not take place between the five ascending generations from mother's side. They practise child marriage where the marriage age is ten years for a boy and eight years for a girl. *Ana* (return of the bride) takes place five to six years after marriage. Marriage is settled by negotiation and they practise monogamy. Though junior levirate and junior sororate are allowed, only junior sororate is in practice. A married woman ties *ganthi* (marriage pendant) round her neck as her marriage symbol. They have practice of *dej* (bride price) in cash which ranges from rupees two to five hundred. A girl after marriage, goes to live with her in-laws but stays at her parents till the *ana* is performed. They grant *fargati* or *chutta-cheda* (divorce) to both men and women. The *gnyat panch* (traditional council) gives verdict in divorce. Whosoever approaches for divorce, he or she has to pay rupees three to five thousand as fine for breaking the marriage. The divorce compensation is given to the aggrieved party. The post-divorce maintenance has to be as per the decision given by the *gnyat panch*. They allow *natra* (remarriage) which takes place between a widow, widower and the divorcee. Dowry has taken place of bride price due to increase in education. The marriage age is also increasing taking into consideration the fact that child marriage has been an important feature of divorce.

Their institution of family comprises extended and nuclear types. Man and woman are equal partners in day to day economic activities. Respect is duly paid to the elder members of the family especially the women in widowhood. Avoidance relationship is maintained between a son- in- law and mother- in- law, daughter-in-law and father- in- law, with husband's elder brother and younger brother's wife. A woman is supposed to cover her head before the avoidance kins. Joking relationship exists between elder brother's wife and husband's younger brother and with wife's brothers and sisters. Conflict and confrontation in the family erupt after son's marriage and father's death on property matters. They practise the rule of male ultimogeniture for residential land and male equigeniture for other properties. The eldest son succeeds to the authority in the family after father's death. Inter- family linkages are maintained during the life- cycle rituals, economic activities and during the election of *gnyat panch*. It is a customary obligation for mother's brother to bring *maushala* (marriage dress) and gifts for marriage. The significant change in the institution of family is the formation of nuclear family. A Bharwad woman has low status. Women have roles in agricultural activities, animal husbandary, collection of fuel, bringing potable water, social function, ritual performances and religious practices. *Fui* (father's sister) has an important role to play during the *babri* (tonsure) ceremony.

Khor-bharo is the pre-birth ritual performed in the seventh month of pregnancy, to ward off evil eye, and the expectant mother goes to her parents house for the first delivery. Elderly female members and *dayan* (local trained midwife) attend the delivery, cut the umbilical cord and bury it behind the house. *Pachora* is the first post-birth ritual performed on the fifth day after birth when the child and mother are given bath. They observe birth pollution for thirty days and after completion of *sutak* (ritual pollution) period, *barse* (naming) is performed. They name the child after procuring the *rashinam* (zodiac name) from the *bhateda* (priest). The maternal uncle performs *babri* (tonsure) to the male child after the completion of one year. *Fui* (father's sister) collects the hair and disposes off in the water. While maternal uncle presents a she goat to the child, *fui* receives a *lugra* (saree) from her brother. Taboos and restrictions are maintained during the menstruation for four days. Marriage is settled by negotiation with the initiative of the boy's father with the help of maternal uncle which is called as *machhi-tadi*. Marriage is finalised and *dej* is fixed. *Adarni* (betrothal) takes place one to even five years prior to marriage at the bride's residence. Milk and butter milk are served in the presence of the *gnyat* people. Marriage is a matter of few days which starts with the installation of *mandva* (marriage booth) and erection of the pole, which are made of *sami* tree, in the booth representing the *gotrej* (*gotar* deity) for *shantek* (worship). *Pithi* (mixture of turmeric powder and groundnut oil) is rubbed on the bodies of both the bride and the groom at their respective houses. A *chouri* (square) is made in the booth for the sacrificial fire. *Mamu* (maternal uncle) of the groom brings *maushala* (gifts) on the same day while *mamu* of the bride brings that on marriage day. The *jan* (marriage procession), with the groom, leaves for the bride's village on the second day. There they are given *janiwas* (separate lodging) on their arrival. The groom, with the *jan*, arrives at the bride's house in the evening where he is led to the *mandava* and is seated on a wooden plank. The bride is also led to the *mandava* and is seated opposite to the groom. *Hast- milap* is performed when the hands of the bride and groom are joined by the priest and *jaimal* (exchange of garland) is performed. *Kanyadan* is performed when the bride is handed over to the groom by the bride's father. *Mangal fera* is performed thereafter. When both the bride and groom are led to the *chauri* in *mandava* and the hems of their clothes are tied together and both walk four times round the sacrificial fire in *chauri*. The groom, while walking, pushes the pot of rice on the completion of every round and finally both sit side by side. The bride's mother ties *ganthi* (marriage pendent) round the neck of the bride. After the religious rites are completed, the couple chews betel and spit on each other, as a mark of new relationship. With this the marriage ceremony concludes. The groom with his wife and *jan* returns to his village next day. The bride returns to her parents after five days. *Ana* (return of the bride) takes place after the girl attends puberty and the consummation of marriage takes place at the groom's residence. Death marks the end of life span. They cremate their dead with the exception of children upto two years and death caused by small pox, who are buried. The eldest son acts as the chief mourner. In case of the death of a married woman, she is dressed in her traditional marriage dress before the cremation. Ashes and bones are collected after cremation and disposed off in running water. They observe death pollution for eleven days. On eleventh day the chief mourner, with the *gotar* members, shaves the head and moustaches. *Shradh* is performed on twelfth and thirteenth days with the help of Kayatia Brahman. *Gotar* members are fed on twelfth day while community dinner is given on thirteenth day. *Barshi* is performed after the completion of one year after death and *gotar* dinner is given.

Traditionally they are a pastoral community. Their present primary occupation is animal husbandry. They rear cow, buffalo and she-goats and sell milk and milk products to their consumers in the different villages and urban areas in exchange of cash and kind on daily and monthly basis. Agriculture is the secondary occupation which has been adopted recently. Agricultural activities among these people are based on the production of crops, mainly at subsistence level. The agricultural implements possessed by them are indigenous. They are mainly dependent on rain. The crops calendar is divided in the three parts viz. *siara* (winter) for *tur* and *moong*, *unadu* (summer) for rice and *jowar* and *chaumasa* (rain) for *ragi*. Apart from these they also produce vegetables. Other means of their livelihood is working in different government organisations.

Their socio-political mechanism is regulated by their *gnyat panch*, the traditional caste council. The council is headed by a Patil and assisted by a *karbhari* and three *sabhya* (members) who are elected by voice vote, the election criteria being the age of the man, his popularity among the community and knowledge of the wordly affairs of the community. Social offences pertaining to adultery, elopement, divorce, inter- caste marriage and disrespect towards the traditional norms are dealt with by the Patil. The offender is readmitted in the community after he or she has hosted a feast and paid the cash fine imposed by the Patil. Implementation of various development welfare activities is the responsibility of modern statutory panchayat. If they fail to resolve disputes, the Patil takes the help of Sarpanch.

The Bharwad profess Hinduism. They worship all the Hindu deities but their favourite deity is Lord Krishna who is the community deity. Memai is their *gotar* deity who is worshipped during marriage, birth and before harvesting of paddy. They consider Mahalaxmi temple, located in Dhanu taluka of Maharashtra and Bindravan temple of Lord Shiva, as their major sacred centre. The Brahman specialises in conducting all their sacred activities. He performs the life cycle rituals and helps in paying homages. Their major fair includes Mahalaxmi fair at Dhanu, held in the month of April and organised on Holi day, Shivaratri fair at Palsana in Gujarat and Holi Mela organised on Holi day at Lavacha in the territory. Their main festival, Kali Chaudas which lies during Navratra in October, is observed. A she-goat is used for worship at this occasion. They also celebrate the other Hindu festivals viz. Diwali, Holi, Diwasa, Rakshabandhan and Akha Teej. They believe in spiritual power and the *bhagat* takes care of it. They are devotees of Swami Narayan panth and visit the temple at Gune in Ahmedabad. *Satiyo* (floor-design) and *garba* folk dance are their non-materialistic elements of culture which are common to all other Hindu communities. The folk songs of marriage, birth and religious festivals are sung in Kathiawadi dialect.

They supply milk and milk products to other communities. Brahman is invited as their sacred specialist. They accept water and *pucca* food from the Brahman, Rajput, Vania, Kapadia and Agri. They share temple, water resources with others and have their own crematorium. Adoption of Swami Narayan Panth has provided them the route of modern linkages with the other communities. They participate along with others, in marriage and religious fair. Cultivator-labour relationship exists with the Dubla and Dhodia. The community has teachers and members holding white collar jobs.

They have a positive attitude regarding the development programmes. Literacy has gone up among the boys who study upto Secondary level and drop out due to economic reasons and start earning to support their family. Girls study upto Primary level and drop out from their studies due to social reasons. Child marriage is also one of the important factors. They make use of both the traditional medicine and modern medicare. They adopt family planning programme but prefer to have three children. They avail of the facilities of drinking water from wells and hand pumps. Electricity, mid-day meal for the children and mother-infant care are available under Integrated Child Development System, so is the facility to purchase cattle under Integrated Rural Development Programme and ration shop. They make use of chemical fertilizers and organic manure in the subsidised rate of 40%. The region has a good network of roads for transportation and communication. The other media of mass communication are radio, cinema. They use fire wood, cowdung cakes and kerosene oil as their fuel. Their attitude towards savings is not favourable and they have to depend on money-lenders and shopkeepers in times of their need.

N.K. Sinha

REFERENCES

Campbell, James M., *Hindu Tribes and Castes of Gujarat*, Vintage Books, Gurgaon (Haryana), Vol. II, p. 267, 1988.

Enthoven, R.E., *Tribes and Caste of Bombay*, Vol. I, 1920, Bombay, The Government Central Press, Reprint, Vol. I, 1975, p. 188, Cosmo Publications, Delhi.

Sherring, M.A., *Hindu Tribes and Castes*, Vol. II, 1879, Calcutta, Spinks & Co., Reprint, Vol II, p. 277, 1974, Cosmo Publications, Delhi.

CHAMAR

The term Chamar has been derived from the Sanskrit word 'charmakar' meaning one who does leather work. They are also known as Rohit. They recall their origin from the religious saint Rabi Das, who was also a Chamar. Briggs (1920-30), Russell and Lal (1975-405) and Campbell (1988-345) have stated that the Chamar claim to have a mixture of Rajput blood and in proof of their descent bear Rajput names. Some of the clan names of the Chamar are similar to those of the Rajput which supports the above statement. They consider themselves synonymous with the Khalpa of Gujarat as they are also associated with the occupation of tanning. They are spread in the villages of Amli, Vagchipa, Demni, Naroli. Their total population according to Census of India 1971 is 635. Chamari is their spoken dialect and the script is Gujarati. They are also conversant with Gujarati and Hindi. They are a Scheduled Caste community.

They are non-vegetarian who they take fish, eggs and meat of goat and fowls. Their staple food includes rice, *jawar*, pulses of *tur* and *mag* (green gram). They use groundnut oil as their cooking medium. They consume plenty of locally available seasonal vegetables. They consume fruits occassionally. Only men consume alcoholic drinks which are available in the local market. They also take milk and milk products. They are fond of smoking *bidi*, cigarettes and chewing betel. *Lapsi* (paste like preparation of wheat flour, ghee and sugar) and nonvegetarian dishes are their special food preparations, which are consumed during betrothal, marriage and other occasions.

The Chamar are divided into fifty exogamous divisions, the *kur* (clan), which are based on territory or occupation, and the clans borrowed from other communities. Out of these only five class are found in the Territory. They are Rathor (a Rajput clan), Banjar (from Banjara), Dhuliya (drummer), Rangari (tanners) and Mochi (leather work). There is no hierarchy among them. The main function of clan is to regulate their marriage alliances and to trace descent. They suffix Rohit to their names claiming the origin from saint Rabi Das. They perceive their position as the lowest in the social hierarchy and consider themselves superior only to the Koli Dhor. They are aware of varna system and recognise their place as Sudra in varna order.

They marry within the community. The rule of exogamy is applied to *kur* (clan), village and to the extent that a marriage cannot take place within the three ascending generations from both the father's and mother's sides. They practise child marriage when the age for a boy ranges from twelve to fourteen years while for a girl from ten to twelve years. Marriage is arranged by negotiation only. They follow the rule of monogamy. A married woman uses *senthi* (red vermillion) on her hair parting and *kali-kanthi* (marriage pendant) as her marriage symbol. They have practice of *dej* (bride price) in cash which is fixed only during the negotiation and paid during the betrothal. After marriage a girl goes to live with her in-laws. *Fargati* (divorce) is granted to either of the spouses by the *samaj* (traditional council). The reasons for divorce are adultery, maladjustment and cruelty. Patels (chief) of both the villages of the wife and husband assemble at the bride's village. The kins are also invited. Whosoever approaches for divorce has to pay the fine and bear the expenditure incurred in the fixing of divorce. Divorce compensation is given to either of the parties as decided by the *samaj*. Children stay with their mother after divorce. The Chamar allow *natra* (remarriage) between widow and widower and the divorcees. A divorced man can marry an unmarried girl while a divorced woman cannot marry a bachelor boy. A widow also can marry the younger brother of her deceased husband. Adult marriage and matrimonial relation with the Chamar of Pardi and Umbergaon in Gujarat are the changes taking place in the institution of marriage recently.

There are extended and nuclear types of family. Members living, eating and working jointly in a house are considered to be a *kutumb* (family). Men and women are equal partners in everyday activities including finances of households. Due respect is paid to elderly members of the family, specially to the widows. It is a customary obligation of sister's husband to play the role of *anwar* (accompanier) and mother's brother to bring *maushale* (marriage dress and gift) in one's marriage. The maternal uncle performs *babri* (tonsure). They have prescribed kinship usages viz. avoidance and joking relationships which are not specific to the community, but common to all other Hindu communities. All sons get equal share in father's property. Eldest son succeeds the authority. Inter-family linkages are sought during life cycle rituals and during the election of Patel (head) of *samaj*. The Chamar women has low status in the society. No rights of inheritance is granted to them. Though their involvement in economic activities is important, they do not have decision making power. Their activities include collection of fuel, bringing potable water, as well as participating in economic activities, social function and ritual performances. They also contribute to family income by working in government offices. *Fui* (father's sister) plays an important role during *babri* ceremony.

Srimant is the pre-birth ritual performed in the seventh month of pregnancy to ward off evil eye and the expectant mother leaves for her parent's house. Elderly female members of the family attend the delivery with the help of *dai* (locally trained midwife). *Chhatti* is the post birth ritual performed on the sixth day after birth. Both the mother and infant are given bath and delivery room is cleaned. *Kur* (clan) deity is worshipped and impression of hand with *sinthu* (vermillion) mixed with water is put on the wall of the delivery room to protect the child from evil eye. *Nampari* (naming) is not a big ceremony. Usually father and some other male relatives give name to the child on fifteenth day. They observe birth pollution for fifteen days. *Babri* (tonsure) ceremony is performed after the completion of one year. Maternal uncle performs *babri* and father's sister collects the hair and disposes off in running water. *Chandla* (betrothal) takes place at the bride's residence one month to one year prior to marriage and *dej* is paid. This is followed by *shankar pada* at groom's house when the bride's father visits the groom, gives presents and puts *tilak* (red mark) on his forehead. Marriage is an event of three days. *Bhagat* (priest) from their own community officiates the marriage. The three day rituals start with the erection of *mandap* (marriage booth). *Grahshantek* (clan deity) is worshipped on second day and the maternal uncle brings *maushala* (marriage gift) in the night. *Pithee* (mixture of turmeric powder) is rubbed on the bodies of the both for three days at the respective houses. The *jan* (marriage procession) proceeds to the bride's house on the fixed day where they are given *janivas* (separate lodging) on their arrival. The groom with *jan* arrives at the bride's house in the evening where he is received by the bride's brother's and his wife. Both the groom and the bride are brought to *chauri* (sacrificial fire) in *mandap*. *Bhagat* from the groom's side performs the marriage rituals. The principal rituals of marriage are *hast-milap* (joning of hands of both), *jaimal* (exchange of garland), *kanyadan* (handing over of bride) and *mangal fera* (circumambulance seven times round the *chauri* by both). Bride's mother ties *kali-kanthi* (marriage pendent) around the bride's neck and puts vermillion on her hair parting. Marriage feast is given by the bride's parents. The groom with his bride and *jan* returns to his village next day. Consumation of marriage takes place at the groom's residence. The bride returns to her parents after three to five days. *Ana* (return of the bride) takes place after she attains puberty. The Chamar cremate their dead. Children below two years and those died of small pox are buried. Eldest son acts as chief mourner. *Tiji* is performed by the *bhagat* three days after death to pacify the departed soul and *daru* (liquor) is served. *Uthmada* is performed on the fourth day after death when clan members are again called and *daru* is served. They observe death pollution for eleven days. *Barhwa* is performed on the twelfth day by the *bhagat* when brothers and sons of the deceased shave their head and moustaches. *Bhagat* with the help of drummers pacifies the departed soul. *Kur* (clan) dinner is given in the night. Now, there is a practice of calling a Brahmin priest to perform the marriage rituals in place of *bhagat*.

Traditionally they are tanners of the skin of dead animals. Only the Chamars of Dapada village are owning agricultural land. Leather work and agriculture are their present day primary occupations. Labour and government services are other means of their livelihood. Leather is mainly made from the skin of buffaloes and cows. They purchase the raw materials of the dead animals from the Koli Dhor and Kathodi communities. They make shoes and chappals after the process of tanning and colouring the animal skin in brownish colour. They sell the leather products from their shops at Silvasa in cash. They also visit the weekly *hat* (market) in Dadra and Naroli villages. Their agricultural activities include the production of crops, mainly at subsistence level. The agricultural implements are indigenous. They are mainly dependent on rain. They grow rice, *jowar*, *ragi* and vegetables. The labourers working in farm and industry receive their wages in cash. They go upto Vapi for doing labour in industries.

Social control is fully regulated by Rohit *Samaj* (traditional council) at district level, headed by a Patil (chief) and assisted by a *karbari* (assistant) from each village, who are elected by voice vote, the election criteria being the age of the man, his popularity among the community-members and his knowledge regarding the worldly affairs of the community. The Rohit Samaj takes care of the social problems pertaining to adultery, deviation from the traditional norms, divorce, remarriage and inter-family disputes. An offender is excommunicated. Cash fine and drink party are the other forms of punishment imposed by the *samaj*. The community feels that the *samaj* has weakened due to growing awareness among the young generation. Implementation of various plans and welfare development activities is the responsibility of modern statutory panchayat.

They profess Hinduism and their main object of worship is Lord Shiva. *Gotrej* is their *kur* (clan) deity. They also believe in spiritual power and *bhagat* from their own community mediates to pacify the *bhutars* (spirits). They also take the help of the Varli *bhagat*. Some times the spirit of the deceased man or woman causes harm to its own family by haunting the house, which is detected by the *bhagat* who tries to ward off the evil spirit. The sacred specialists are from their own community who attend their life cycle rituals and religious practices. They also call the Brahman priests to officiate their marraige. Amba Mata temple in Gujarat, Shiva temple at Udhawada and Brindavan and Mulganga at Nashik are their major sacred centres. They also believe in other tribal deities namely *baghiya* (tiger god) and *chandiya* (moon god). Shivaratri fair at Palsana and Holi Mela at Lavacha in Gujarat are their main fairs. They do not have any specific festival of their own but celebrate the Hindu festivals of Diwali, Janmashtami, Holi and Raksha Bandhan. The Bhowada festival of the Kokna is also rejoiced by the Chamar. They are active followers of the Jai Gurudev sect initiated by Shri Muktanand Swami at Ganeshpur in Maharashtra with aims and objectives of self realisation and getting rid of bad habits. Their art is represented by their leather products and their colouring. *Satiya* (floor design), *tarjawana* (tattooing) and *garba* folk dance are the non-materialistic elements of culture which are common to all other communities of the territory.

They accept water, *kachcha* and *pucca* food from the hands of all the communities except the Koli Dhors. They have their own crematorium and drinking water resources. They visit temple alongwith others. They participate with other communities in the Holi *mela* at Lavacha and Bhowada festivals of the Kokna and Varli. The services of *bhagat* from Varli and Brahman priest are required to officiate sorcery and marriage. Symbiotic relationship exists with the Koli Dhor on whom they depend for the skin of dead animals. Their services are required by the Varli, Parsi and Christian to work on the fields. They have businessmen, members holding white collar jobs, teachers and engineers. Their political leadership has emerged at panchayat level.

The Chamar have a positive attitude towards the development programmes. Literacy has gone up both among the boys and the girls. Generally boys study upto college level but drop out as they have to start earning to support their families. Girls study upto secondary level and drop out mainly due to social reasons, early marriage being one of them. They avail of the facilities of health and medicare but make use of both the indigenous and modern medicines. They favour family planning programme, and use modern family planning methods. They generally prefer to have three children. They avail of the facilities of drinking water, reservation in recuruitment, Integrated Rural Development Programme, mother- infant care under Integrated Child Development Scheme through Balwadi, and ration distribution system. They make use of electricity, chemical fertilizers at subsidised rate of 50% and also of organic manure.

N.K.Sinha

REFERENCES

Ballal, K.D., *Dapada : A village in Dadra and Nagar Haveli*, Registrar General, Delhi, Census of India, 71 Series I, Part VI-C : 1974.

Briggs, W.G., *The Chamars*, B.R. Publishing Corporation, Delhi, P. 31 : 1920.

Campbell, James M., *Hindu Castes and Tribes of Gujarat*, Vintage Books, Gurgaon (Haryana) Vol. II, p. 345 : 1988.

Census of India, 1971, *General Economic, Social and Cultural table*, Series-27, Part III, A & B, Part IV-A, Delhi, 1974.

Russell, R.V. and H. Lal, *Tribes and Castes of the Central Province of India*, Vol. II, 1916, London: Macmillan and Company; Reprint, Vol. II, p. 405, Cosmo Publications, Delhi, 1975.

DHODIA

The Dhodia, one of the Scheduled Tribes, are also called Dhodi. The community does not have any legend of their origin except that they are the descendants of the Rajput prince of Kathiawad. They migrated to Dadra and Nagar Haveli from Gujarat. Antonio Francisco (1904-128) has discussed about their inhabitation (Dadra and Nagar Haveli was a Pargana of Daman till 1954). Shah (1954-19) writes "the term Dhodia might have been derived from 'dhur' or 'soil' because the tribe is essentially agricultural, or it seems to have been derived from Dhullia, a town in west Khandesh, from where they might have migrated. According to Roy and Rizvi (1985-48) the Dhodia trace their origin to Lord Krishna. They further state that the progeny of Dhan Singh and Roop Singh, the Rajput princes of Saurashtra and Lini and Chhan, the Naika sisters were later said to be the Dhodia. They are spread in the villages of Naroli, Amli, Samarvani and other 32 villages. The total population of the Dhodia is 10,270 (Census of India 1971 part X-A&B, series-28, page 11-13). Dhodi is the spoken dialect within the community and Gujarati is their script. They also converse in Gujarati with others.

Bio-anthropological information on the Dhodia is available in the study carried out by Joshi (1978) and his team. This has been discussed in Appendix I.

They are non-vegetarian who take the meat of goat, rabbit and fowls. They also take fish, crab and eggs. Rice, *jowar* and wheat form the major contents of their food. They also consume pulses of *tur* (red gram) and *mag*. The consumption of locally available vegetables is high. Fruits viz. *kela* (banana), *jamrukh* (guava), *keri* (mango) and berries are taken occasionally. *Daru* (alcoholic drink) and toddy are consumed by the men folk daily. They also take beverages like tea, milk and butter milk. *Dhokra* (stuffed fried bread), *lapsee* (pastelike preparation of wheat flour with ghee/oil and sugar/jaggary), *pia*, *sira* (porridge) and *dudh-*

pak (rice boiled in milk) are the special food preparations made on festive occasions.

They are divided into nine exogamous divisions based on *kurh* (clan) namely Banjaria, Bariya, Parsi, Mehta, Dari, Fudosi, Velgarahi, Bilarkhaw, Attara, Atti Mulgarahiya. Some of the clan names show the existence of totemism among them, e.g. Mul Garahiya (name of goat), Bilarkhaw (named after cat) etc. Enthoven (1920 : 330) has discussed fortytwo exogamous sub-divisions of the Dhodia living in Gujarat and Maharashtra. Roy and Rizvi (1985 : 55) have discussed about 183 exogamous divisions of Dhodia of Gujarat based on *jut* (clan). The basis of differentiation of the *kurh* is social. The main function of these divisions is to regulate their marriage, to trace their descent and to participate in the life cycle rituals. There is no hierarchy among them. They consider themselves superior to the Varli, Kokna, Dubla, Koli Dhor, Kathodi, Makrana and Chamar. They are not aware of the varna system.

The Dhodia resort to community endogamy and *kurh* exogamy. They practise adult marriage. Marriage is settled by negotiation and in few cases also by mutual consent. They practise monogamy only. Pre-marital sex is forbidden. If it happens with a girl from the community and from different *kurh*, the girl is married, after imposing fine on the boy by the Patil of *samaj*. *Kanthi* (marriage pendant) is the marriage symbol for women. They have practice of *dej* (brideprice) which is paid in cash. A girl after marriage goes to stay with her in-laws. *Fargati* (divorce) is granted to both men and women by the Patil (head). Whosoever approaches for divorce, he or she has to pay fine imposed by the *samaj* Patil (chief of traditional council). In case of a woman seeking divorce, she has to pay back the bride price with the divorce fine. It is ascertained from the man and woman that they are not willing to live together. The amount of the fine goes to *samaj*. The usual grounds for divorce are adultery, maladjustment, cruelty and insanity. *Natra* (remarriage) is allowed between widow and widower and the divorcee. It is also allowed in case of *devarbatu* (junior levirate). Regular form of marriage is fully resorted. In every case a social sanction is needed from the *samaj*.

Kutum is the local term for family. Extended and nuclear families are common among them. It is a part of the kinship obligation of the brother to take care of his sister (specially after divorce and in widowhood) and widow mother. *Bhawad* (sister's husband) and mother's brother play the role of *anwaro* (accompanier) and brings *maushala* (customary marriage gift) in marriage. Avoidance relationship is maintained between a woman and her *jethu* (husband's elder brother), *vavai* (father-in-law), *vevai* (mother-in-law). A *bahu* must keep her head veiled before the kins with whom she observes avoidance. Joking relationship is maintained between *deyar* (husband's younger brother), *bhabhi* (elder brother's wife) and with *nanai* (wife's brother's wife). Conflict and confrontation in the family starts after son's marriage and father's death, on property matters. They follow the rule of male ultimogeniture for residential land and of male equigeniture for other properties. Eldest son succeeds the authrority after father's death. Inter-family linkages can be envisaged during life cycle rituals, economic activities and during the election of *samaj* Patil.The significant change in the institution of family is the formation of nuclear family. Dhodia women have a low status. Right of inheritance is not granted to them. They are generally busy in agricultural work, collection of fuel, bringing potable water, social function, ritual performances and religious practices. They also contribute to family income by doing labour jobs in agriculture. They do not have any role in politics. *Fui* (father's sister) plays an important role during *panchro* (fifth day birth ritual), *barse* (naming) and *babri* (tonsure) ceremonies.

The life-cycle rituals are common to all Hindu communities of the territory.

Land is the major economic resource which is under control of individual proprietors. They are a landowning community. Their primary occupation, the tradition of which still continues, is terrace cultivation and allied activities. Nonskilled labour, fishing, trapping, toddy tapping and government services are other means of their livelihood. Traditionally they held the land as tenants of the Rajputs, Parsis and Christians whom they paid revenue after collecting it from the Dhodias. The tenant had to pay 1,000 *escude* (Portuguese currency) as the annual rent to the landlord. Apart from that, half of the total products went to the landowner. The system was called *rokar ganat* and *khand* system. The Land Tenancy Act, 1971 was introduced on 1.5.74 after land survey in 1964 and reforms were carried out, making provision for only one sixth of the produce to go to the landowner. The surplus land was taken by the government and was distributed to the landless and the Dhodia became the landowners. The agricultural implements possessed by them are indigenous. They mainly produce paddy, *ragi*, *tur* and *mag*. They also grow seasonal vegetables. They are mainly dependent on rain water. A few of them avail the facility of electric pumps. They sell the vegetables and surplus products directly in the market of Silvasa and tribal weekly market in cash. The Dhodia, working as agricultural labourer, get their remuneration in cash as well as in kind. Development of industrial complex, facilities of job reservation and IRDP are the part of changes took place in their economic life after liberation.

Social control is regulated by their *samaj* (traditional caste council). The community has a two tier system of council viz. the council at *parha* (hamlet) level headed by the *karbhari* and *samaj* at village level headed by a Patil. The Patil is elected by the *karbharis* of different *parhas* by voice vote. A *karbhari* takes care of the social problems at *parha* level, while the *samaj* deals with the problems not solved by *karbharis* specially the inter-community marriage, premarital sex, adultery, divorce, betrothal and remarriage. *Gnyat-bar* (excommunication) and *dand* (cash fine which ranges from two to five thousand), are the forms of punishment imposed by the *samaj*. Plan implementation and development activities is the responsibility of modern statutory panchayat. Though the introduction of statutory panchayat has reduced the authority of traditional council, the *samaj* still has control over their social system.

The Dhodia follow tribal religion. They believe in supernatural as well as the spiritual powers. Brahmdev who is prominent among all of their deities, is their family deity. They also worship Hanuman and Mahadeo. They make offerings to their deities on Sunday. They worship their ancestors and prepare images from wood which are called as Khatradev. Their other deities are Samra Dev (deity of cholera), Kakawalia (deity of small pox), Sitla Mata (deity of measles), Pet-fodi-Mata (deity of evil eye), and Kansari Mata (deity of corn). They also believe in *bhutars* (spirits) to whom a small quanitity of food and drinks is offered on every feast. The *bhua* (magico-religious specialist) is responsible for protecting from the malevolent spirits, to mediate between them and the deities and to cure from the prolonged diseases. He is one of the most respected person in the village through whom the forces of evil spirits and sorceries are countered. Their main festival is Divaso associated with the *dingle-dingla lagan* (mock marriage) carried out by the young unmarried girls. The youngsters get acquainted with the marriage rituals through the observance of their festival. They also celebrate the other festivals namely Vagbaras, Diwali, Holi and Dussera. Their main sacred centre is the temple of Samradeva, located at Rudvel village in the Chikhali Taluka of Gujarat where they pay homage between Kartika and Falgun months. Their main fair is Shivratree *mela* at Palsana.

They have musical instruments and *chundar* (tattooing), *Tur* (double headed drum) and *thali* (brass plate) are their traditional percussion musical instruments used during marriage and on other festive occasions. The female folk have the *chunder* work on their arms, wrist and chin with red and black pigments. *Gheriya* is the folk dance, in which both men and women participate along with relatives; and separately (with strangers) during Divaso and marriage. The different types of tune and steps in the dance is called *chal*.

The Dhodia had landlord-tenant relationships with the Mauri Rajputs, Christian, Parsi and Khoja when the land-tenure system prevailed. They take the services of Dubla, Kokna and Varli, as agricultural labourers. They consider themselves good Hindus and accept water, *kachha* and *pucca* food from the Mauri Rajput, Kapadia, Agri, Kahar, Varli, and Kokna. They accept only *pucca* food from the Dubla. They consider the Chamar, Kathodi and Koli Dhor as unclean and lower in rank and do not accept food from them. They also do not dine with the Christian, Parsi, Khoja and Makrana. They have their own crematorium and temple. They share water resources with others. *Dharm bhai* (putative kinship) is maintained with the Dubla. The community has teachers and members holding white collar jobs. The community leadership has emerged at the level of village panchayat.

They avail of the educational facilities where both the boys and girls study up to college level and then drop out, to start earning to add to the income of their family. They make use of both the traditional and modern medicare. Though their attitude towards family welfare programme is favourable, they still prefer to have four children. They avail of the facilities of drinking water through dugwell and pipes, irrigation by tubewell under Integrated Rural Development Programme. They also avail of the facilities such as mid-day meal for children, Integrated Child Development Scheme, ration distribution system, self-employment, organic manure and chemical fertilizer. Firewood, cowdung cake and kerosene oil are their fuel media. They are exposed to radio, cinema, etc. They are served by a voluntary organisation such as Vanbasi Kalyan Ashram.

N.K. Sinha

REFERENCES

Census ofIndia, 1971 Part X-A, A & B, Series-28, Controller ofPublications, Delhi, p. 113, 1974

Enthoven, R.E., *Tribes and Castes of Bombay*, Vol I., 1920, Bombay, The Government Central Press, Reprint, Vol I., p. 33, 1975, Cosmo Publications, Delhi.

Roy, Shibani and Rizvi, S.H.M., *Dhodia Identity*, B.R. Publishing Corporation, Delhi, p. 48: 1985.

DUBLA

The Dubla are also called Halpati. The name Dubla is said to derive from the Sanskrit word "durbal" meaning weak which refers to their economic hardship. The term *halpati* (master of plough) was adopted by them after liberation, after Halpati of Gujarat. Shah (1958 : 124), Raghavaiah (1970), Enthoven (1920 Vol. I : 341), Antonio Fransisco (1904:128) and Sinha (1983) have confirmed this interpretation about their origin. They are believed to have their origin from Rajput because of their connections with Gujarat. Besides Daman they are also spread in the Surat and Valsad districts of Gujarat. Their total population, according to Census of India 1971, is 1,443. Dubli is their dialect and Gujarati is the language as well as the script used by them. Besides Gujarati they are also conversant in Hindi. The community has the constitutional status of a Scheduled Tribe.

They are non-vegetarian and their food habits include rice, *jowar*, wheat and pulses such as *thur* (red gram) and *mag* (green gram). They take tea and buttermilk and eat fruits occasionally. They consume alcoholic drinks and toddy which they consider as digestive. The special food viz. *puri*, *lapsee*, *sira*, *potoya* and *biriyani* is prepared on the festive occasions. They are fond of smoking *bidi*, and chewing tobaccoo and betels.

They are divided into two subgroups namely Talavia and Karchha. The two endogamous subgroups are divided into five exogamous *kurh* (clan) namely Rathod, Gangaria, Damania and Sarvaria. They do not know much about their subgroups or units and their inter-connection. They lost their surnames during the Portuguese regime and started suffixing 'Halpati' to their names after the interaction with the Dublas of Gujarat. They consider themselves superior to the Chamar, Kathodi, and Koli Dhor. The rule of exogamy is applied to the *kurh* and no marriage can take place with the four ascending generations from both the father's and mother's side. They practise adult marriage. *Kariganthi* (marriage pendant) is the marriage symbol for married women. Marriage is both by negotiation or self-arranged and the form of marriage is monogamy. *Dhej* (brideprice) is paid both in cash and kind. Patrilocal and neolocal are the rules of residence for them. *Fargati* (divorce) is granted to both by the traditional council. It is ascertained from the husband and wife whether both are not willing to continue living together. While granting divorce, a certificate is prepared in duplicate signed by the husband, wife and witnessed by the *nyat panchas* (members) of both the sides. Whosoever approaches for divorce has to pay divorce fee as per the decision of the *samaj* Patil and this remains in the account of the *samaj*. Brideprice is returned to him. The common grounds for divorce are adultery, cruel treatment, neglect of household jobs, inability to bear a child and witchcraft. The post-divorce maintenance is the responsibility of woman's parents/brother. *Natra* (re-marriage) takes place through *devar-batu* (junior levirate) and *sare-lagan* (junior-sororate). A widower marrying a virgin girl, can resort to the regular form of marriage. A widow can marry again in the presence of *samaj* (traditional council) in her village. Adult marriage in place of child marriage, matrimonial relations with the Dubla of Gujarat and Daman, self arranged marriages and rise in divorce due to industrial development at Silvasa and Vapi in Gujarat are the forms of changes that took place after liberation.

Kutumb is the local term for family. Extended and nuclear families are common among them. Men and women are equal partners in day to day life. The relations between husband and wife are good. Avoidance relationship is maintained between a woman and her husband's elder, wife's elder brother/sister, *aja* (husband's mother) or parent-in-law and all those who belong to the upper generation of her husband. A woman covers her head outside her house whenever she happens to meet her avoidance relatives. Joking relationship is maintained between *devar* (husband's younger brother), and *bhabhi* (elder brother's wife), with *bai* (husband's sister), with *chali* (wife's younger sister) and *chala* (wife's younger brother). Kinship obigation towards brother, sister, (specially after divorce or in widowhood) and widow mother are followed in the family. Sister's husband has the prescribed role of *anwario* (accompanier) and *mama* (mother's brother) has to send the *maushala* (marriage gift) during the marriage. The rules of male ultimogeniture for residential land and male equigeniture for the other properties are practised among them. Eldest son succeeds the *karta* (authority). Inter-family linkages can be envisaged during the election of the *samaj* Patil (traditional council head). The significant change in the institution of family is the formation of nuclear family. Dubla women have low staus in the society and have no right of inheritance. Their roles are restricted to agricultural labour, collection of fuel, bringing potable water and participation in social and religious rituals. They do not have any role in political activities except the right to cast their votes in the periodical elections. This, too, is done in consultation with their male members. They contribute to family income by doing manual jobs in nearby industries and agriculture. *Fui* (father's sister) plays an important role during *chhathi* (sixth day ritual after birth), *nampari* (naming) and *mundan* (tonsure) ceremonies. Sister plays the role of *karvali* (companion) during her sister's marriage. Their life cycle rituals are similar to those of the other Hindu communities of the region.

Agriculture and agricultural labour are their primary as well as the traditional occupation. Jobs in industry, forest and road construction are the other means of livelihood. The landless Dublas were provided land by the Mauri Rajput, Dhodia and Parsi whom they serve. A few of Dublas who own land, have the production just on subsistence level. They produce *chokha* (rice), *jowar* and *val* (a type of nut) and vegetables. They have to depend on their subsidiary occupation to run their households. A small number of Dublas are the tenants of the Mauri Rajput traditionally and two third of the production per season goes to the landlords. The women and children work as the domestic servants. The labourers in agriculture, forest and road construction receive their wages in cash and kind. Abolition of feudal system, provision for the mechanisation of agricultural implements, distribution of land under tribal sub-plan, development of the industrial complex and job reservation have helped the Dublas in improving their economic conditions.

The Halpati Samaj regulates their daily activities within a village and it is headed by Patil who is elected by voice vote. He is assisted by the *karbharis* of different *parhas* (hamlet). The *karbharis* elect their Patil. The *karbhari* takes care of the social problem within the *parha* while the Patil deals with the problem, not solved by the *karbharis*, specially the inter-caste marriage, pre-marital relation, adultery, divorce, betrothal and remarriage. *Nyatbar* (excommunication) and insistance on a community feast are the forms of punishment imposed by the *samaj*. An offender expiates after providing the community dinner. Planning and implementation of welfare and developmental activities is the job of modern statutory panchayat. Their political organisation has undergone a change after liberation. The periodical elections have revived factions among the Dublas but it has not succeeded in replacing the system of social control by the Halpati samaj.

The Dubla follow tribal religion. Their religious belief and rituals recognise the existence of two different sources of supernatural power namely the spirits and the deity based on the Hindu mythology. Braham Dev is their caste deity who looks after them and to whom they attribute a pre-eminent position among all the religious beings. Dev is their house deity. Holi Mata is their hamlet deity and Ashper Dev is their village deity. Other deities are Malhwada Mata, Sitla Mata (goddess of small pox), Mohabhu Mata (deity of pimples), Akashi Mata (deity of sky who protects children from evil eye), Bamania Bhoot (king of spirits, residing near crematorium), Petfori Mata (protects from abortion), Kaka Waliya (deity of small pox), Marki Mata (deity of plague), Kansari Devi (deity of corn) and Khokholi Mata (deity of cough). Dev (house deity) is worshipped on every festive occasion and during any auspicious work. The *bhagat* or *bhua* (magico-religious specialist) is responsible for performing all the magico-religious practices for protecting them from the malevolent spirits, mediating between the Dublas and their deities and curing the prolonged diseases. He is one of the most respected persons in the village who is supposed to have special power, through which the forces of evil spirits or sorceries are countered. They also worship the Hindu deity viz. Lord Shiva and Hanuman. Their main festival is *Divaso* associated with the *dingli-dingla lagan* (mock-marriage) ceremony by the unmarried girls. It signifies that every Dubla girl expects to marry and observance of this festival provides acquaintance with the marriage rituals. It is celebrated between Jeth-Ashadh (Hindi calendar months) and the date is fixed by the Patil. They also celebrate the Hindu festivals like Navratra, Holi, Diwali, Makar Sankranti and Dussehra with full vigour.

They have their musical instruments and the tattooing marks. *Sarangi* (violin) is a stringed instrument played for recreation and made by themselves with bamboo stick and hair of buffallo. Skin of the frog is used to make the strings of the violin. *Chundar* (tattooing marks) is a mark which men and women get made on arms and hand, with red and black pigments. It is done with a fine needle or a thorn of *babul* (accacia) with the help of a mixture of lamp black, a decoction of beawood bark and juice of green leaves of *val* (creeper). After tattooing, turmeric powder, which is supposed to have antiseptic effect, is applied to the portion punctured and the person is advised not to apply water to the parts of the body so as to prevent painful swelling. The most commonly used tattoo marks include *buneli* (mark), *choful* (leaf-shape mark), *morle* (peacock), portrait of the deities and self name. *Tur-thali* (percussion musical instrument) is the main folk dance performed by men and women during marriage and Divaso.

The Dublas work as *hali* for the Mauri Rajput, Dhodia and Parsi. They accept water, *pucca* and *kachha* food from the Rajput, Kapadia, Kahar, Dhodia, Kokna, Varli and Agri. They consider the Chamar, Kathodi and Koli Dhor as unclean and lower in rank and do not dine with them. They consider themselves as good as other Hindus and do not accept food from the Makrana. They have their own water resources, crematorium and temple. They are allowed to enter the kitchen of the above mentioned communities due to their long association and economic inter-dependence. Many of them hold white collar jobs. Periodical elections of statutory panchayat and assembly, landlord-tenant relationship, employer-worker relationship in agriculture and industries provide the chance of modern linkages with other communities.

Their attitide towards the development programme is positive. The literacy level has gone up. Boys study up to college and drop out as they have to earn to support their family. Girls drop out also due to social reasons. They avail of the facilities of primary health centres, family welfare, drinking water, training centre for self-employment through Industrial Training Institute, free electricity, mid-day meal for the children in the school and mother and child-care under Integrated Child Development Scheme, public distribution system and revised rate of minimum wage policy. Dublas, who own the land, make use of chemical fertilizer and insecticides which they get from the government agencies. Being economically weaker they have to depend on their landlords and employers when they need money. For agriculture, they mainly depend on rain water. Cowdung cakes, firewood and kerosene oil are their fuel resources. They are exposed to mass communication through radio, cinema.

N.K.Sinha

REFERENCES

Enthoven, R.E., *Tribes and Caste of Bombay*. Vol I, 1920, Bombay, The Government Central Press, Reprint, Vol I., p. 341, 1975, Cosmo Publications, Delhi.

Franscisco, Antonio., *Notices-E-Documentas-para A Historia De Damao*. Bastora (Goa), Vol. II p. 128 : 1904.

Raghavaiah, V, *Tribal Revolt*, Andhra Rashtra Adimjati Sevak Sangh, Vellore, 1971.

Shah, P.G., *The Dubla of Gujarat*, Bhartiya Adimjati Sevak Samaj, Delhi, 1958.

Sinha, N.K., 'Dubla Ethnography. Structure and Process'. Unpublished report submitted to A.S.I., 1983.

KAHAR

The Kahar are also called Raj Bhoi. They claim to be one of the sub-divisions of Gujarat Bhoi and descendants of Rajputs. They attribute the name Kahar to a *palki* (litter) carrier. According to Enthoven (1920, Vol. I, Page 181) the term Bhoi, besides being the name of the caste, is also used to denote a litter bearer and has subsequently been appropriated by the members of the other castes pursuing the same occupation. This statement has been supported by Sherring (1974, Vol. II, Page 119 & 199), Thurston (1906, page 167), Bahadur (1981 Page 2) and Russell and Lal (1916, Vol. I, & III, Page 350 & 291). According to their legend they first migrated from Lucknow in the United Province, during the British war with Nawab Wazid Ali Shah, to Gujarat and finally settled at Silvasa. They are spread in Silvasa and also in Gujarat. Gujarati is the language as well as script used by them. Besides Gujarati they are also conversant with Hindi.

Their staple food includes rice, *jowar*, pulses of *tuar* (red gram) and *moong* (green gram). They also consume locally available seasonal fruits and vegetables. Groundnut oil is used for cooking purposes. Only men take alcoholic drinks which they purchase from the market. *Puri* (fried bread), *lapsi* (preparation of milk), wheat flour and sugar or jaggery) and *sira* are their special food preparations made on the festive occasions. Alcoholic drinks are a recent addition.

They are divided into eleven exogamous divisions based on *got* (clan) out of which only five, namely Bhagat, Kahar, Baxiwala, Hukkawala and Nataviya are traceable. The main function of *got* is to regulate marriage alliance. They have started suffixing Dass to their names recently. They are well aware of the varna system and recognise their status as Vaishya. They perceive their position inferior to that of the Brahman, Rajput, Kapadia and Agri and superior to the Parsi, Makrana, Dhodia, Dubla, Varli, Kokna, Kathodi, Chamar and Koli Dhor in regional social hierarchy. They marry within the community. The rule of exogamy is applied to the *got* level and a marriage can not take place within the three ascending generations from both the father's and the mother's side. Earlier practice of child marriage which has changed to adult marriage where the age for a boy ranges from 20 to 25 years and for a girl 18 to 20 years. Marriage is settled through negotiation only and they do not allow self arranged marriages. If a boy or a girl is found to be indulging in pre-material sex, he or she is excommunicated. The form of marriage is monogamy. A man can marry his wife's younger sister only after his wife's death. A married woman uses *kali-ganthi* (marriage pendent) and *kanku* (vermilion mark on forehead) as her marriage symbols. *Dej* (dowry) is paid in kind which is fixed during the negotiation. A girl after marriage goes to live with her in-laws. *Chhutta chheda* (divorce) is granted to both men and women by the *samaj* (traditional council). The reasons for divorce are adultery, inability to bear a child and cruelty. *Samaj* does not ask for any fine but whosoever approaches for divorce, has to give a feast to the *samaj*. The husband breaks the *kali-ganthi* from his wife's neck which indicates the discontinuation of his claim over her. If adultery is proved against either of the spouses, the compensation, fixed by the Pramukh (head), is given to the aggrieved party. Post-divorce maintenance is taken care of by her parent or brother. They allow *natre* (remarriage) to widow, widower and divorcees. No *kali ganthi* is tied in *natra*, only *kanku* is applied to the divorcee in front of the *samaj* and her parents. In widow marriage, the rituals are performed by her parents. The rituals viz. *hasta-milap*, *jai-mal* and *mangal-fera* are performed and the man takes the widow with him as his wife.

Their family is both of extended and nuclear types. They have prescribed kinship usages. Avoidance is maintained between a mother-in-law and son-in-law, a daughter-in-law and father-in-law, with husband's elder brothers and younger brother's wife. A woman keeps her head covered in front of the avoidance relatives. Joking relationship is maintained with husband's younger brother, with elder brother's wife and with wife's sister and brothers. Conflict and confrontation in the family arise after son's marriage and father's death on property matters. All sons get equal share in the property after father's death. Eldest son succeeds the *karta* (authoritarian) after father's death. In case of no male issue, *dattak* (adoption) is done of brother's or sister's son. Sister's husband plays the role of *anwar* (accompanier) and maternal uncle brings *maushala* (customary marriage gift) in the marriage. Though women assist their men in day to day life, they have low status. Their roles restrict to collection of fuel, bringing potable water, social and ritual functions, religious practices and participation in economic activities such as purchasing fish from the Machchi of Daman and sale in the daily regulated market for cash. *Fui* (father's sister) plays an important role during *bal-kapwani* (tonsure ceremony).

The life cycle rituals for birth, post-birth, naming, *mundan*, marriage and death are common to all the Hindus of the territory. They observe birth pollution for forty days and death pollution for ten days. Marriage is solemnised at the bride's residence and is consummated at the groom's residence. Brahman is called to officiate at their life cycle rituals.

The Kahar are a landless community. As stated earlier their traditional occupation was carrying palanquins and litter which has now shifted to fishing and manual labour. The reason for their migration from Gujarat to Silvasa is not kncwn but it is presumed that the Kahar might have been recruited by the Machhi of Daman (Dadra and Nagar Haveli was a part of Daman till 1954) as labourers in fishing trade. Purchasing the fish from the Machhi of Daman and selling in the territorty is still their primary occupation. Service in government offices, industries and shopkeeping are their other means of livelihood. They also sell dry fish which they purchase from Daman. They do their transaction in cash at Silvasa while at the weekly traditional market in kind also.

Their social life is regulated by Kahar samaj (traditional council) at village level. The council is headed by Pramukh and assisted by a *karbhari* (manager) and five *sabhyas* (members). The office bearers are elected by voice vote. The tenure of the office bearers is for three years. The Bargam Kahar Samaj at regional level stopped functioning some forty years ago. Social problems pertaining to adultery, remarriage and divorce are dealt with by the *samaj*. Excommunication is the form of punishment imposed by the *samaj*. In changing situation, the position of *samaj* has weakened and the Pramukh does not enjoy respect of the new generation. Plan implementation and development activities are the role of modern statutory panchayat.

The Kahar profess Hinduism and are followers of Sanatan Dharma. They worship all the leading Hindu deities and celebrate the major Hindu festivals. Their favourite deity is Ambaji which is also their village deity. The *got* deities are termed as *gotrej*. They are worshipped during life cycle rituals. Mahalaxmi temple at Dhanu in Thana district of

Maharashtra and Jalaram Temple at Birpure in Gujarat are their major shrines. They fulfil their *vadha* (promises) after performing *mundan* at the Mahalaxmi temple. Brahman are their religious specialists who perform their life cycle rituals and help them with religious offerings and homages at the places of worship. Their major fair is Mahashivratree fair held at Palsana in Gujarat. Gokul Asthami is their main festival which falls in Shravan month. Diwali, Navratree, Holi and Shivratree are other festivals which they celebrate with full vigour. They do not have any art of their own. *Satiya* (floor design) and *garba* (folk dance) are common to other Hindu communities.

They maintain traditional linkages with the Machhi of Daman so far as their occupation of selling fish is concerned. Services of Brahmans are required during life cycle rituals. They accept water, *pucca* and *kachha* food from the hands of the Brahman, Rajput, Kapadia and Agri but do not allow even the Brahman to enter their *rashoda* (kitchen). They share water resources, temple and crematorium with the Rajput, Kapadia and Agri. They visit the temple of Mahalaxmi and participate in Diwali, Shivratree and Holi festivals with others. Relationship is maintained with the Machhi of Daman for the purchase of dry fish. The community members are holding white collar jobs.

Their attitude towards the development programme is favourable. The literacy level has gone up. Boys study upto graduate level and drop out as they have to start earning to support their family. Girls study upto primary level and drop out as they are economically weak and they also have to assist their parents. They make full use of modern medicare. Though they favour family planning and use modern methods of family planning, they prefer to have four children. They get safe drinking water and are self employed through dry fish trade. Mother and infant care under Integrated Child Development Scheme and ration distribution system is available to them. They also get electricity. Firewood, cowdung cakes and kerosene oil are their fuel resources. Construction of metalled roads within and outside the territory has provided means of transportation and trade links with the neighbouring areas. Their savings are not large and they have to depend on shopkeepers for their needs.

N.K. Sinha

REFERENCES

Bahadur, K.P., *Caste, tribes and culture of India*, Ess Ess Publications, New Delhi, Vol. VII, p. 4:1981.

Enthoven, *Tribes and Castes of Bombay*, Vol I., 1920, The Government Central Press, Bombay, Reprint, Vol I., p. 181, 1975, Cosmo Publications, Delhi.

Russell, R.V., and Hira Lal, *Tribes and Caste of Central Province*, Vol I & III, 1916, London, Macmillan and Company, Reprint, Vol I & III, pp. 305 & 291, 1975, Cosmo Publications, Delhi.

Sherring, M.A., *Hindu Tribes and Castes*, Vol. II, 1879. Thakar Spinks & Co., Calcutta (3 Volumes), Reprint, pp. 199 & 284, 1974, Cosmo Publications, Delhi.

Thurston, E., *Castes and Tribes of Southern India*, Vol. I, 1909, Madras, Government Press, Reprint, Vol. I, p 267, 1975, Cosmo Publications, Delhi.

KAPADIA

The Kapadia are also called Kapadi. They are divided into four sub-groups based on occupation namely Tamboli, Patel, Kapadia and Panwala. No information is available in the existing sources on their origin and migration. They believe that they migrated from the adjoining areas of Gujarat, and have settled in the region during the Portuguese regime. They are scattered in the villages of Vagchipa, Khilwani and Silvasa and have also spread to the adjoining areas of Gujarat. Gujarati is their language and script. They also speak Hindi.

They are purely vegetarian and their staple food is rice, wheat, *jowar*, and the pulses of *tuar*, *mag* and *urad*. They consume locally available seasonal fruits. Groundnut oil is their cooking medium. They take beverages like milk, tea and butter milk. *Puri* (bread)), *lapsi* (paste like preparation of wheat flour, sugar and ghee), *dhokla* and *dudh-pag* (rice boiled in milk) are special food preparations made on the festive occasions.

The Kapadia are divided into seven exogamous sub-divisions based on *kurh* (clan) namely Patelia, Mahadevia, Jhal, Jhalavia, Kabulia and Kathi. There is no hierarchy among the sub-divisions. The main function of *kurh* is to regulate the marriage alliances and to trace their descent. They suffix Kapadi to their names. They consider themselves to be inferior to the Brahman, Mauri Rajput and Vania and superior to the Agri, Kahar, Bharwad, Parsi, Kokna, Varli, Dhodia, Dubla, Chamar, Koli Dhor, Kathodi and Makrana, in the social hierarchy. They are well aware of the varna system and recognise their place in the Vaishya order.

They marry within the community and the subgroups. The rule of exogamy is applied to *kurh* and marriage cannot take place within the five ascending generations from both the father's and mother's sides. They practise adult marriage and the age at marriage ranges for a boy from 25 years to 28 years while for a girl from 22 to 25 years. The marriage age of eighteen years for girls and twenty years for boys has gone up thanks to higher education. A man can marry his wife's sister after her death. Marriage is settled through negotiation. Sex before marriage is not tolerated. If a girl commits sexual offence with a community man both are punished through fine and readmitted in the society only after getting purified by a Brahman. Though polygamy is allowed, they only practise monogamy. *Kanthi* (marriage pendent) is the marriage symbol for a married woman. Practice of *dej* (dowry) in kind exists, which is fixed during the negotiation. A girl, after marriage, goes to stay with her in-laws. They do not allow divorce. *Natra* (remarriage) is permitted between a widow and widower. Self arranged marriage, inter-subgroup marriage, increase in marriage age are some of the recent changes.

Families are both of extended and of nuclear types. They have prescribed kinship usages. Avoidance relationship is maintained between mother-in-law and son-in-law, a daughter-in-law and father-in-law, with younger brother's wife and with husband's elder brother. Women are expected to cover their heads in front of those with whom they observe avoidance. Joking relationship exists with the husband's younger brother, elder brother's wife, wife's sister's and brother's. Sister's husband plays the role of *anwar* (accompanier) during marriage. All sons get equal share in the property after father's death. Eldest son succeeds as the head of the family. Inter-family linkages are fully envisaged during the life cycle rituals and during the election of *samaj* Pramukh. A Kapadia woman has a low status. Role of a woman is restricted to agricultural activities, collection of fuel, bringing potable water and social and religious functions. They also contribute to family income by doing jobs. Father's sister has an important role during naming, *babri* (tonsure) and bringing *maushala* (marriage gift) during marriage. Sister plays the role of *kureli* (accompanier) to the bride in marriage. Conflict and confrontations arise between the sons after the father's death in property matters. The tension sometimes extends to the breaking of extended family into nuclear ones.

Srimant is the pre-birth ritual performed in the seventh month of pregnancy when Lord Ganesh is worshipped and the expectant mother leaves for her parents' house. Elderly female members attend the delivery, assisted by *dayan* (locally trained midwife). *Chhathee pujan* is the post-birth ritual performed on the sixth day after birth. The room is cleaned and purificatory bath is given to the mother and infant in the day time. A piece of white paper with betel leaf is kept in the room in the night. It is their belief that Goddess Saraswati visits the child in the night and writes the fate on the child's forehead. The infant is adorned with white dress which is considered auspicious. *Nampari* (naming) ceremony is performed on eleventh day by the *fui* (father's sister) after procuring the *rashinam* (zodiac name) from the Brahman. The child is placed on a *jhori* (portable cradle of cloth) and held by four girls from four sides singing after which the child is placed on a wooden cradle. The *sutak* (ritual pollution) runs for 39 days. On fortieth day after birth, the mother visits the temple, and thereafter she is allowed to start her household activities. *Babri* (tonsure) is performed to the male child after one or three years. Some times it is performed even on a day before marriage, if it is not performed in early age. They prefer to perform *babri* at the temple of Mahalakshmi in Maharashtra. A girl is confined for five days during her menses. Marriage negotiations are initiated by girl's parents. *Chandla* (betrothal) takes place a fortnight prior to marriage at groom's residence and *dej* (dowry) in kind is fixed. Marriage ceremonies go on for three days starting with *mandav-mahurta* (erection of marriage booth) on the first day. *Pithi* (mixture of turmeric powder and groundnut oil) is rubbed on the bodies of the bride and the groom by sister-in-law at their respective houses for three days. *Ganpati* is installed on the second day. *Kurh-devi* is worshipped for *griha-shantek* and *kurh* (clan) dinner is given. *Ukadau* is performed at both the hosues in the early morning before sunrise to call the unwanted evil near the waste land outside the house with the belief that on marriage even unwanted person should be invited. It is performed on third day at the bride's residence. *Fui* (father's sister) brings *maushala* (marriage gift) in the night. The *jan* (marriage precession) leaves for the bride's village on third day in the afternoon where they are given *janiwas* (separate lodging) on their arrival. The groom with the *jan* arrives at the bride's house in the evening and is received by the bride's mother, called *otara*, and is led to the *mandva* and seated there facing the east. The bride is brought by the maternal uncle and is seated opposite the groom. A curtain is held between the two and *hast-milap* (joining of hands) of the both is performed by the priest. Curtain is removed thereafter and *barmal* (exchange of garland) is performed. *Kanyadan* (handing over of the bride) is performed by the bride's parents amidst the recitation of verses by the priest. *Mangal fera* is performed thereafter when the bride and the groom make four rounds of the sacrificial fire lighted in *chauri* (square) in *mandva* where first three rounds are led by the bride and the fourth round is led by the groom; then both are made to sit side by side. *Kanthi* (marriage pendent) is tied round the neck of the bride by her mother. This is followed by *pehramni* (gift by the relatives) and worship of the clan deity. Marriage dinner is given by the bride's parents. The groom with his bride and *jan* leaves for his village on the fourth day. *Ana* (return of the bride) takes place on third day after marriage. Comsummation of marriage takes place at the groom's residence. They cremate their dead. Children below five years and those who died of small pox are buried. Eldest son acts as the chief mourner. Ashes are collected after cremation and disposed off in running water. They observe death pollution for ten days. The chief mourner and the *kurh* members shave their heads and moustaches on the eleventh day and perform *anjurhi* to mark the end of pollution. *Sradh* (ancestor worship) is performed on twelfth day when the articles designated for the use of the departed soul and *sidha* are presented to the Brahman and community dinner is given. *Barshi* (memorial rite) is performed after completion of one year. Life cycle rituals are curtailed in the course of time, as it has become more and more expensive to observe them.

Land is their main natural resource. There are both landowners and the landless. The control of land is with individual proprietors. Agriculture is their traditional occupation. In present days kirana business, grocery, agriculture and transportation are their primary occupations. Service in different government offices and industry are other means of their livelihood. Production of crops is at subsistence level. Their agricultural implements are indigenous. They are mainly dependent on the markets of Bulsad and Pardi (both in Gujarat) for their provisions which they purchase with the cash transaction. They sell the provisions in the daily regulated markets. The kirana merchants also visit the *hat* (market) located in the tribal areas. Labourers, workers in industries receive their wages in cash.

The social control is under the Kapadi samaj (traditional caste council) at regional level. The *samaj* was earlier functioning at village level at Silvasa. After independence, Vapi is also included in the samaj. The samaj is headed by a Pramukh who is elected by voice vote. He is assisted by a *karbhari* (accountant) and five or seven or eleven *sabhyas* (members). The samaj takes care of the problems pertaining to marriage, inter-caste marriages, premarital sex, remarriage, economic assistance to the poor men from community and distribution of books to the poor students. An offender is excommunicated. He or she can be readmitted to the community by paying fine, as imposed by the Pramukh. Plan implementation and welfare activities are the jobs of modern statutory panchayat.

The Kapadia profess Hinduism. They worship all the Hindu deities but Hingraj Devi which is the community deity has a special place. *Gotrej* is their *kurh* (clan) deity has a special place which is worshipped during birth, marriage and *athem* in Magh month.Ganpathi is their village deity. They consider the temple of Hingraj Devi at Gandevi in Gujarat and Mahalakshmi temple in Maharashtra as their major shrines of pilgrimage. Their specialist is the Brahman who helps them in life cycle rituals, paying homages and performing religious rituals. Their major festivals are Maha Athem and Nag Panchami. They also celebrate the other Hindu festivals viz. Bhaibeej, Janmashtami, Diwali, and Holi. They have recently formed an organisation called Kapadia Samaj Shanti Panth associated with religious activities of the community and which also deals with social reforms. The meeting of this organisation is called every year at different places. The elements of art viz. *satiya* (floor design), *tarjawana* (tattooing), *garba* and *ras* dances are common to all other Hindu communities. Only women participate in the folk dances.

They accept water and *pucca* food from the hands of the Brahman, Mauri Rajput and the Vania of Vapi . They do not accept *kachha* food from others. They exchange *sidha* with others during their activities in *hat* (local market). They share well and water resources, temple and crematorium with others. They participate in the marriages of the Brahman, Mauri Rajput, Agri and Bania. The services of a Brahman are sought for the life cycle rituals and religious performances. Cultivator-labour relationship is maintained with the Dhodia and Dubla. The occupation of kirana and transport business has provided them the chance of modern linkages with all the communities in and outside the territory. The community has businessmen and engineers. Their political leadership has emerged at village panchayat.

Literacy level has gone up both among the boys and girls. Boys study upto college and drop out from studies as they have to earn to support their family. Girls study up to secondary level and drop out to get married. They make full use of modern medicare. They favour family planning programme but prefer to have three children. Drinking water facility is available to them through dug wells and pipes. Self employment, irrigation with tubewells, mother-infant care under Integrated

Child Development Scheme and ration distribution system are available. They use electricity, organic manure and chemical fertilizers. The region has good network of roads which provides the means of mass communication. Being traders, they encourage savings.

N.K.Sinha

KATHODI

The Kathodi are also called Kathkori. According to them, the word Kathodia is derived from the Marathi word *kathod* which means skin cleaners. Another explanation is that the term Kathodi has been derived from the Marathi word *kath* which means catechu. Not much information is available in the existing sources on their origin except Campbell (Vol. 15, 1988-319) who has described the Kathodia as the catechu-makers who originally came from north Konkan. According to them, they are migrants from Maharashtra who were brought by the Parsi for liquor manufacture and catechu production and also to work as agricultural labourer during Portuguese regime. They are spread in the villages of Amboli and Dapada of the territory. Somehow, they are also scattered in Maharashtra and Gujarat. Their total population according to Census of India, 1971 is 334 which has decreased from 1005 in 1961. Kathodi and Kokni are their dialects with the admixture of Marathi and Gujarati languages within the community. They also speak Kokni and Marathi languages and use Devnagari script. They are a Scheduled Tribe.

They are non-vegetarian who eat the meat of goat, *lawi* (bird), *shashla* (rabbits) and fowls. They also eat pork and carrion. Their staple food includes rice, *jowar*, *nagli*, pulses of *tur*, and *urad*. They also consume roots viz. *teeri*, *tumoy*, and tubbers viz. *kalihan*, *jeri*, *lunda* and tender bamboo sprouts which they collect from forest. They are very fond of *daru* (home made liquor) which is one of the reasons for their degraded economic condition. They smoke *bidi* which they make themselves with tobacoo and leaf of *sunghai*. They use *chakmak* (a type of traditional lighter) to light *bidi*. They also chew betel. Groundnut oil is their cooking medium. *Shovela* and *kanji* (gruel) of *jowar* and *nagli* are their special food preparations made on the festive occasions.

They are divided into five exogamous divisions, namely, Bhoia, Wagh, Sura, Paghi and Panwar which are based on *kurh* (clan). The *kurhs* are associated with the totemic object. The basis of differentiation is social. They suffix their *kurh* to their names. The main function of *kurh* is to trace their descent and to regulate their marriage alliances. They are not aware of the varna system. They regard their own position inferior to the Rajput, Brahman, Kapadia, Agri, Kahar, Kokna, Varli, Dhodia, Dubla, Parsi and Makrana and superior to the Chamar and Koli Dhor.

They marry within the community. The rule of exogamy is applied to *kurh* level. They allow consanguineous marriage with father's sister's daughter and mother's brother's daughter. A man can marry his wife's younger sister after her death. They practise adult marriage. Marriage is settled by negotiation, by *khandariya* or *gharad* (marriage by service) and and by mutual consent. The mode of *khandariya* is practised by the Kathodi who can not pay *pend* (brideprice) and have no money. The *khandar* serves at the bride's parents for a stipulated period of three to five years and marries the girl and becomes the *ghar-jamai.* In such a marriage all the expenses are borne by the bride's parents. If a girl becomes pregnant before marriage and delivery takes place after marriage, the child is considered legal. *Pend* (brideprice) is paid only in kind which includes two *mund* of *bhat* (paddy) and four *piyali* (an unit of measurement) of *kath* or pulse. A married woman ties *ganthi* (marriage pendent) around her neck as her marriage symbol. A girl after marriage goes to stay with her in-laws. *Chhutta* (divorce) is granted to both men and women by the *samaj* (traditional council). The reason for divroce are adultery, impotency, cruelty and insanity. If a woman approaches for divorce, she has to pay back the expenses incurred in marriage. In case of the insanity no amount is paid. In case of charges of adultery proved against the wife, *dawa* (repayment of brideprice) is desired by the husband. The husband breaks the *ganthi* (marriage pendant) from his wife's neck, during the divorce which indicates he would not have any claim over her as his wife. *Bed-utaru* (remarriage) is allowed to widow, widower and divrocee. No *ganthi* is tied in remarriage. A feast is given to *samaj* and man takes the woman as his wife. If a girl runs away with a boy from other community she is excommunicated

The prescribed general kinship usages viz. avoidance and joking relationship are maintained within the family members. Avoidance is maintained up to the extent that women cover their head in front of avoidance relatives. It is obligatory for a brother to look after his sister if she becomes a widow or divorcee. A *khandar* is also admitted to the family. Maternal uncle has an important role to play during *babri* (*tonsure*), and brothers during marriage. Conflict and confrontation arise after father's death on property matters. After father's death the widow inherits half of the property and remaining is equally shared by the sons. In case there is no male issue the remaining half of the property is equally shared by those daughters who were married through *gharad*. Eldest son succeeds the authority. Though men and women assist each other in day to day life, women have low status. They have roles in animal husbandry, collection of fuel, roots and tubers, bringing potable water, economic activities, ritual performances. They also contribute in family income by doing mannat jobs.

The life cycle rituals are similar to those of the Kokna, Varli and Koli Dhor. Marriage-rituals can take place in either of the houses generally depending on the economic condition of the person. Death rituals and religious practices are officiatied by the *bhagat* of the Varli or Kokna.

Forest and land are their major economic resources, though they are a landless community. Their traditional occupation is tanning of dead animal's skin. As it has been discussed earlier they were brought by the Parsi landlords to work as agricultural labourers in their fields and to prepare catechu and *daru* (homemade liquor). Agricultural labour continues to be their present day primary occupation. They worked as *kharchi-khandel* (bonded labour) with the Parsi landlords. While women worked as domestic maid servants in their houses, men worked in the fields. During peak agricultural season, women are also engaged in the fields. Besides the low status of labourer, *daru* (liquor) is another factor which has caused further degradation. Charcoal and catechu productions are their other occupations. They visit the Dang district of Gujarat for the charcoal and catechu production on contract basis with the Jangal Society for seven to eight months. Remaining four to five months they work under Parsi landlords. They were provided residential land by the Parsis in their field. They get two meals and some cash as their remuneration under the contract. Few were given lands as tenants, by which arrangement they get one third of the production. It was only after Land Reforms Regulation Act, 1971, that the surplus land of the Parsis was taken over by the government and distributed among the landless. They were freed from the clutches of the Parsis after the implementation of the Bonded Labour Abolition Act and were provided two acres of land by the Land Reform Office. They were also given the financial assistance of Rs. 500/-per individual i.e. Rs. 100/-cash and agricultural implements, seeds and fertilizers. They were brought from Surangi and Tulavali villages and rehabilitated in Amboli village and were provided 12' x 24' residential land. Presently they work as agricultural labourers on contract basis. Labour work in forest is their other means of livelihood. They receive their wages in cash and kind in agricultural activities and for the forest work, they get cash. Their economic condition improved in the 80's.

Social control is exercised by their *samaj* (traditional council) at village level, headed by Patil (head) who is elected by voice vote. The tenure of Patil changes after every three to five years. The daily activiteis and disputes over cattle, land, divorce and adultery in the village are under the Patil's control. Efforts are made to resolve even criminal assault within themselves, failing which they approach the Patil of the Parsi. Before liberation they never thought of approaching the government or judiciary as the cases were referred to Daman, Diu and being poor it was not possible for them to defend themselves through legal means. Cash fine and feast were the forms of punishment imposed by the Patil. Plan implementation and developmental activities are the responsibilities of modern statutory panchayat. The political awareness brought about the change; they now have an *agyavan* (leader) who looks after the government's developmenal programmes and get them acquainted with the facilities provided to the Scheduled Tribes.

They follow traditional religion of the tribals. Their folk belief is associated with the totemic objects and spiritual powers. Hirwa Dev and Pitar are their *kurh* deities who are worshipped during lifecycle rituals. Wagh Dev (tiger god) is their village deity who is worshipped once in a year when *sindur* (vermilion) is applied and goat is sacrificed. The *bhagat* from the Kokna or Varli is invited to officiate at the rituals. The Kathodis simply watch the rituals and get their due share after sacrifice. They also worship the Hindu deities viz. Mahadeo and Uma of wider pantheon. *Bhagat* from the Varli or Kokna community pacify the *bhutar* (ghost). Their major festival is Shun; and main fair is Holi fair at Lavachha. They also celebrate the Hindu festivals namely Diwali, Holi and Akhateej. Their art is represented by *tarjwana* (tattooing) and *cholu* (folkdance). Both men and women participate in folk dance. They use *chang* (flute), a wind instrument and *dhol* (drum) and *kadi* (beater) a percussion musical instrument. Folk songs are sung during marriage and *cholu* dance.

They maintain traditional linkages with others, specially the Parsis at economic level, even when they worked as bonded labourers. Though they are freed from the bonded labour now, they still work for them in agriculture on contract basis. A Kokna or Varlli *bhagat* is invited to perform death and other religious rituals. They accept water, *pucca* and *kachha* food and *sidha* from the hands of all the communities except the Koli Dhor. Wagh Dev is the village deity, which is common to other tribal communities in the village. They participate in the Holi fair at Levachha with the Kokna, Varli, Dhodia, Dubla and Koli Dhor. They share the crematorium and water resources with the Kokna and Varli. Work-interaction exists with the Kokna and Varli. Patron-client relationship exists with the Parsis, cultivator-labour relationship exists with the Parsis, Kokna, Varli, Rajpur and Dhodia. They have teachers within their community.

They have a positive attitude towards development programmes being implemented after independence. Boys study upto secondary level and drop out as they have to start earning to support their family. Girls do not study because they are poor and have to support their family. They make use of both the traditional and modern medicare. They do not favour family planning and prefer to have four or more children because more children will provide assistance to the family members. They avail of the facilities of primary health centre, drinking water through rivulets and dug-wells, provision of loan cum subsidy for animal husbandry under Integrated Rural Development Programme, seeds, chemical fertilizer and other agricultural assistance from Large Size Multipurpose Cooperative Society and Primary Agricultural Credit Soceity after 1982, right of conservation under social forestry, pre-primary education, mid-day meal for children, child and mother care under Integrated Child Development Scheme, distribution of agricultural land and residential land under Indira Awas Yojna, ration distribution system. They get free electric supply by the administration. Fire-wood and kerosene oil are their fuel resources. They are exposed to mass communication through radio, cinema, etc. They are in touch with various government agencies, voluntary agencies like Vanvashi Kalyan Ashram at Khanval and political parties. They have to depend on landlords and shopkeepers in their need, specially during marriages and other festive occasions.

The Kathodi were provided agricultural land, after they were freed from bondage and were rehabilitated in Manipada of Amboli village under NREP. In all fifty houses in 12' x 24' area were constructed under

Indira Awas Yojna where the Kathodi themselves worked for the completion of the Yojna.

N.K. Sinha

REFERENCES

Ballal, K.D., *Socio-Economic Profile of Dadra and Nagar Haveli*, Census of India, 71, Registrar General, New Delhi, Series-1, Monograph No. 2:1974.

Campbell, James, M., *Hindu Castes and Tribes of Gujarat*, Vintage Books, Gurgaon, (Haryana), p. 319 : 1988.

KOKNA

The Kokna are the third largest tribe of the Territory. Little information is available in the existing sources about their origin. They recall their migration from Konkan in Maharashtra. Ballal (Census of India, 71, part VI-C page-23), referring to Enthoven states, "they are one of the hilly tribes from Thana and were driven northwards from Konkan by the pressure of the Great Durga famine in 1396-1408 AD". They are divided into two religion based endogamous groups namely the Kokna and the Christian Kokna. They perceive their distribution in the sixty villages of the Union Territory. They are also spread in Gujarat and Maharashtra. Their total population according to Census of India 71, is 9,928. Kokni is their spoken dialect and script is Devanagri. They use Gujarati language and script in their dealings with others. They dress like the Varli. They are a Scheduled Tribe. Bio-anthropological information is available on the basis of the studies carried out by Joshi et al., (1978) which has been discussed Appendix I.

They are nonvegetarian, who eat the meat of goat, *lawi* (a bird), *shashla* (rabbit) and fowls. They also take dry fish, land crabs and locally available seasonal vegetables. Their staple food includes rice, *jowar*, pulses of *tur* and *urad*. Groundnut oil is used for cooking boiled rice and pulse. They also consume roots namely *teers*, *tumou* and tubers namely *kodakan*, *jeri*, *lunda* and tender bamboo sprouts which they collect from forest. They are fond of drinking toddy and *daru* (home made alcoholic drinks). They smoke *bidi*, cigarette and chew betel. They make *bidi* themselves with tobacco and leaf of *sunghai*. They use *chakmak* (a type of traditional lighter) to light *bidi* and cigarette. *Shavle*, *khichri* and *kanji* (gruel) of *jowar* (prepared after grinding and boiling in water) are their special food preparations for the festive occasions.

The two endogamous divisions of the Kokna, mentioned earlier, are divided into a number of *kurh* (clan) namely Mohla, Gait, Choudhary, Chauhan, Bhoia, Gavli, Gayanwad, Thorat, Mahankali, Ganghurha etc. Those names are based on the totemic objects and have similarity with those of Rajput clans. The basis of differentiation of the aforesaid exogamous and endogamous divisions is social and religious. They suffix their *kurh* (clan) to their names. The main function of *kurh* is to trace descent and to regulate their marriage alliances. They are not aware of the varna system. They perceive their position inferior to the Rajput, Kapadia, Agri, Kahar, Bharwad, Dhodia, Parsi and superior to the Makrana, Varli, Dubla, Chamar, Kathodi and Koli Dhor.

They resort to endogamy prevalent in the community and *kurh* exogamy. They allow marriage with the mother's brother's daughter, the matrilateral cross-cousin. Traditionally they practised child marriage followed by *ana* but now they practise adult marrriage. Marriage is settled by negotiation, *dabra* (mutual consent) and *khandariya* (marriage by service). The inter- tribal marriage between the Christaian converts of Kokna and Varli are based on *dabra*. The mode of *khandariya* is practised by those Kokna who cannot pay *pend* (bride price) and have no land. In such cases, the groom serves at the bride's residence for a stipulated period of three to five years and marries the girl. If he stays with his in-laws after marriage he is called *ghar-jamai*. In this form of marriage all the expenses in marriage, are borne by the bride's parents. If a girl becomes pregnant with *khandar* before marriage and child is born after marriage, it is considered legal. *Pend* is paid in both the cash and kind. The cash amount ranges from Rs. 51/- to Rs. 125/- and the kind includes two *mund* of *bhat* (paddy) and five *piyali* (a unit of measurement) of *kathor* (pulses). A married woman ties *ganthi* (marriage pendant with two beads of alluminium) round her neck as her marriage symbol. A girl after marriage goes to stay with her in-laws. *Fargati* (divorce) is granted to both by the traditional council. The reasons for divorce are adultery, cruelty, and insanity. Whosoever approaches for divorce has to pay some amount as fixed by the patil of traditional council. If a woman approaches for divorce, she has to pay back the expenditures incurred in marriage or minimum of Rs. 500/-

In case of insanity of either of the spouses no money is paid. In case of charges of adultery having been to proved against the wife, *dawa* (repayment of bride price) is demanded by the husband. Extramarital relations are not uncommon among them and if a woman runs away from her husband and stays with her paramour, *dawa* is claimed by her husband. The reunion with other man is socially approved and termed as *natra* or *pat* on which no *pend* is claimed. The former husband breaks the *ganthi* from her wife's neck during the divorce procedure in the presence of *samaj*. During *pat*, drink party is given to the father of the divorced woman and the council. No *ganthi* is tied in remarriage. *Pat-mode* (widow remarriage) is not allowed. A man can marry his wife's sister during his lifetime after consulting his wife. If a girl runs away with a boy from other community, she is excommunicated. There are no separate marriage rules for the Christian Kokna except that they marry within the group and also with the Christian Varli.

They have both extended and nuclear types of families. The prescribed general kinship usages viz. avoidance and joking relationship are maintained within the family members. Brother has to look after his widowed or divorcee sister. A *khandar* is also admitted in family after marriage. He stays with his in-laws. Maternal uncle has an important role to play during *babri* (*tonsure*), so also brothers, during marriage. Conflict and confrontation in family erupt after father's death on property matters. After father's death, the widow inherits half of the property and remaining is equally shared by the sons. In case of no male issue, the remaining property is shared by the daughters who are married through *khandaria*. Eldest son succeeds the authority in the family. Though women assist the men in day to day life, they have a low status. Their jobs are collection of fuel, roots and tubers, bringing potable water, participating in social function, economic activities and religious practices. They also contribute to family income by doing labour jobs in forest, road construction sites and jobs in Anganwadi and schools.

The life cycle rituals of both Kokna and Christian Kokna are similar to those of the Varli except that the Christian converts visit the father of church for seeking blessing after birth and marriage. Traditionally the Kokna marriage rituals were performed at the groom's residence and the *barhardi* (marriage procession) used to bring the *nawri* (bride) to the *nawra* (groom). Now it depends on the economic condition of the party. Marriage rituals are performed for three days as among the Varli. A *toran* of mango leaf and *bambachi pana* is erected in place of *mandwa* where bride and groom sit for marriage. *Shesh* is performed by five married women from the bride's side and five from the groom's when rice and coconut are presented to the bride in her lap and both perform *fera* (making five rounds of the *umar* tree-stick) near *taran*. The consummation of marriage takes place at the groom's residence. The Christian Kokna bury their dead while the Kokna cremate. While *bhagat* officiates at the cremation, the father of church officiates at the burial.

Land and forest are their major economic resources. Land is under control of individual proprietors. There are both landowners and the landless among them. Traditionally they were practising *bhunj* (slash and burn) cultivation. As their settlements are in forests and hilly terrain, terrace cultivation is their present day primary occupation. They now own some land also. This land was given to them by the government from the land acquired from the landlords under the Land Reform Regulation Act. Those who do not own land, do cultivation under land tenure system with the Rajput and Parsi and in return they get their share (i.e. one sixth of the produce goes to the landlord). Before 1954, one third went to the land lord. The Land Tenancy Act 1971 was introduced with effect from 1.5.1974 in the territory.

Their agricultural tools and implements are of indigenous type. They are mainly dependent on rain for irrigation. Paddy, *jowar* and *nagli* are the chief crops produced by them. The tenants pay the landlord both in *rokar ganat* (cash) or *khand* (kind). The quantum of rent is fixed as per the produces and paid after harvesting. They sell their surplus yields to the shopkeepers directly in *adhwara* (tribal weekly market), transacting both in cash and kind. Labour jobs in agriculture, forest, industry, animal husbandry, *mad* (honey) making and government jobs are other means of their livelihood. They also work as labourers and receive their remuneration at the rate of rupees eight or two seers of paddy or *nagli* (madwa) and one time food or three seers of paddy plus one time food. Women receive rupees seven. They worked as *kharchi-khandel* (bonded labour) to the Parsi and Rajput earlier. Though they try to be financially independent, sometimes they have to borrow money for consumer goods, festivals and celebrations; and are expected to clear debt within six months, failing which they have to work in the fields of the creditor. They also do animal husbandry as they look after buffaloes and cows of the Rajput, Agri and other communities and in return they get oxes for three to four months to cultivate their lands.

Social life of the Kokna is regulated by their *samaj* (traditional council) at two levels namely *parha* (hamlet) level headed by a *karbhari* and at village level headed by a Patil. They are elected by voice vote and their tenure changes every year. Patil is elected by the *karbharis* of each *parha* in village. The *karbhari* takes care of the daily activities and disputes over cattle, land, divorce, bride price, adultery and remarriage at hamlet level. If he does not succeed, the Patil is approached. Cash fine and drink party are the forms of *kadi-mudi* (punishment) imposed by the *karbhari* or Patil. Minor criminal issues are also resolved by them at village level. They also approach the Sarpanch of the statutory panchayat in inter-tribal disputes. They consider their Patil to be the final authority, during the periodical elections. Plan implementation of development programmes are the role of modern statutory panchayat.

They profess traditional tribal religion and Christianity. Their folk beliefs and practices are associated with the totemic objects and spiritual power. Hirwa Dev, Pitar, Nirbanshi, Himai Devi are their clan deities who are worshipped during life cycle rituals, Diwali and Holi. Waghya (tiger God) is their village deity and is worshipped once in a year on Krishna Paksha Dwadashi (12th day of dark half) of Ashwin month when *sendur* (vermillion) is applied and goat is sacrificed. Giving a bath to village deity is the job of Patil while the *bhagat* preforms the ritual part. Mahadeo is the deity of wider pantheon. Kansar Devi (deity of grain) and Makar Dev (deity of harvesting) are the other deities. Narsingh Deo is symbolic deity. Christian Kokna visit the church to attend mass as per their convenience but they also believe in tribal deities and *bhagat*. *Bhagat* officiates at their life cycle rituals. He exorcises the evil spirits during illness and pacifies the ghost. *Shun* is their main festival and their main fair is Holi held at Lavachha. They also celebrate the other Hindu festivals viz. Holi, Diwali and Akhateej. They have their own sacred specialist. Their art is represented by their graphic art of painting and drawing, *tarjawana* (tattooing), folk songs of marriage, folk dance and woodcraft. Their folk dances are *bhowada* (in summer), *torpa* and *dhol*. Both men and women participate in *bhowada* and *torpa* dances but *dhol* is the dance of men only, after plantation of paddy and Holi. They use *torpa* and *chang*, the wind instruments, *dhol* and *kadi* as the percussion instrument, during the said dances. They make *torpa* (made of bamboo) with pumpkin, leaves of toddy and *neera*, the gum waste of honey, *gharghari* (rain coat made of bamboo and leaves of palas), *pati* (basket of bamboo leaves), *davli* (small spoon made from pumpkin) and *thala* (wood surface of grinder) themselves.

They accept water, *kachha* and *pucca* food from the Rajput, Brahman, Agri, Kapadia, Kahar, Varli and Dhodia. They accept *sidha* from all the communities except the Koli Dhor, Chamar and Kathodi. They share water resources, crematorium and village deity with the Varli. Inter-community marriage takes place between the Christian converts of Kokna and Varli. They participate with the Varli and Koli Dhor in Holi fair and with the Varli in life cycle rituals. Landlord-tenant relationship is maintained with the Varli, Rajput, Parsi and Dhodhia. Cultivator-labour relationships exist with the Parsi, Rajput and Dhodia. They have members of their community in teaching jobs and their political leadership has emerged at regional level where they have representatives in parliament.

They have a positive attitude towards development programmes. Boys study upto secondary level and drop out as they are poor and have to earn to support their family. Only a few study upto graduate level. Girls study upto primary level and drop out due to social reasons and start earning to support their family. They use both the traditional and modern medicare. Though they are not against the family planning programme, they prefer to have four or more children. They avail of the facilities of health, drinking water through dug well and rivulets, provision of loan for animal husbandry and horticulture on 50% subsidy under IRDP., self employment under NRDP, seeds and other agricultural assistance from Large Size Multipurpose Cooperative Socitеties and Primary Agricultural Credit Society, right of conservation under social forestry, pre-primary education and child and mother care under Integrated Child Development Scheme. They make use of free electricity, chemical fertilizer and organic manure which they get under 50% loan cum subsidy scheme from Block Development Office and Agriculture Department. Fire wood and kerosene oil are their fuel resources. They are exposed to mass communication through radio, cinema etc. They are in contact with extension agencies, voluntary agencies like Vanvasi Kalyan Ashram at Khanvel, Adivasi Social Service Society and Christian Mission, and political parties. Economically weak, they need financial help during festive occasions for which they have depended upon *sauhar* (moneylender) and shopkeepers.

N.K. Sinha

REFERENCES

Campbell, James, *Hindu Castes and Tribes of Gujarat*, Vintage Books, Gurgaon (India). Vol. II, p. 321, 1988.

Ballal, K.D., *Dapada: A Village in Dadra and Nagar Haveli*, Census of India, 71, Govt. of India Press, Delhi, Series - 1, Part VI-C, 1974.

KOLI DHOR

The Koli Dhor are also known Kolga, Korh and Korgha. The term Koli Dhor is associated with the occupation of tanning of dead *dhor* (animal) skin. According to Enthoven (1920 - Vol. II-253) and Ballal (Census of India, 71, part VI C - 23), "they are also called Tokra Koli. Dhor Koli derives from *dhor* meaning cattle because they eat beef and Tokre from *thokar* meaning a bamboo, which refers to their being called bamboo cutters". Ballal (1974:23) also says that Koli Dhor and Kolga are the same people who were grouped together in 1961 census. They trace their migration from Maharashtra and Gujarat about three generations back. They are spread in the villages of Dudhni, Randha, Vedpa and Dapada panchayats of the territory. Somehow they are also located in the neighbouring areas of Gujarat and Maharashtra. Their total population, according to Census of India 1971, is 1,396 which form 2.19% of the total tribal population of the Union Territory. Kokni is their spoken dialect. Their script is Marathi. They enjoy the status of a Scheduled Tribe.

They are non-vegetarian and take meat of goat, fowls, *shasla* (rabbit), *bowl* (wild cat) *tavi* (a kind of bird) and buffalo. Their staple food includes rice, *nagli*, pulses of *tuar* (red gram)and *urad* (black gram). They afford to take fruits regularly. They also consume roots viz. *teeri, tumou* and tubers viz. *kadukan* (a jungle creeper), *jeri* and *lunda* which they pick from the forest. They are addicted to drinking toddy and *daru* (alcoholic drinks). They use groundnut oil as their cooking medium. *Shavele, khichri* (boiled rice and pulses) and *kanji* (gruel) of *jowar* or *nagli* (prepared by grinding and boiling in water) are the special food preparations consumed on the festive occasions. They are fond of smoking *bidi* which they prepare themselves with tobacco and leaf of *sanghai*.

The Koli Dhor are divided into two endogamous divisions namely, Dhor Koli and Tokre Koli. The latter is considered higher in social hierarchy than former on the basis of their occupations. Both the divisions have *kur* (clan) as an exogamous unit. While Dhor Koli have five *kur* namely More, Pardhi, Pipalka, Kordad and Tople, Tokre Koli have three *kurs* namely Mukana, Dalviod and Shinwaj. These exogamous units are based on totemic object e.g. More from *mohr* (peacock). They do not eat peacock but domesticate it. They suffix their *kur* to their names. The chief function of *kur* is to indicate their descent to regulate their marriage alliances and to participate in the life cycle rituals. They are not aware of the varna system. They perceive their position lowest in the regional social hierarchy.

They resort to community and sub-division endogamy and *kur* exogamy. They allow consanguineus marriage i.e. both matrilateral and patrilateral cross cousins marriage. Traditionally they practised child marriage followed by *gaona.* Presently they practise adult marriage and the age of marriage for a boy ranges from eighteen to twentytwo years while for a girl from fourteen to ninteen years. Marriage is settled by negotiation and *khandariya* (marriage by service). *Khandariya* is practised by the Koli Dhor who are unable to pay the *pend* (bride price) and have no land. He settles in bride's village and works for a stipulated period of three to five years and marries the girl. He can return to his village with his wife or stay at the bride's village by becoming the *jamai* (son-in-law) of the village. If he stays with his bride's father, he is termed as *ghar-jamai.* In this form of marriage all expenditure is borne by the bride's parents. Both monogamy and polygamy are permitted. *Pend* (bride price) is paid in kind which includes three *mund* of *bhat* (rice), four *piali* (a unit of measurement which contains four kg. of cereals) of *kathwar* (pulses) and twelve *piyali* of *nagli.* A married woman ties *ganthi* (marriage pendant) round her neck as her marriage symbol. *Chhuttu-chheda* (divorce) is granted to both man and woman, by the traditional council. The reasons for divorce are adultery, cruelty and insanity. Divorce compensation is given to the aggrieved party. *Dawa* (repayment of bride price) is claimed by the man from wife's father only in case of adultery. Extra-marital relations are not rare and if a woman runs away from the husband and lives with her paramour, *dawa* is claimed by her former husband. The reunion with the paramour is socially approved and termed as *natra* (remarriage) in which no *pend* is claimed. The former husband breaks the *ganthi* from his wife's neck in the presence of traditional council which indicates that now he would not have claim over her. During *natra*, a drink is served to the father of the wife and the council. A man can marry her wife's sister after her death or even during her lifetime; if she is unable to bear a child, and gives her consent for the second marriage. Widow or widower marriage is also permitted. In *natra* no *ganthi* is tied.

They have both extended and nuclear types of family. They have prescribed kinship usages. Avoidance relationship is maintained between a mother-in-law and son-in-law, a daughter-in-law and a son-in-law, with younger brother's wife and husband's elder brother. Joking relationship exists with the husband's younger brother, with elder brother's wife, with wife's brother and sister. A *khandariya* is also included in family in case of no male issue. Maternal uncle has an important role to play during *babri* (tonsure) ceremony. Conflict and confrontation in the family erupt after father's death on property matters. They still follow the old Portuguese Law of Inheritance where a widow inherits half of the property and remaining is equally distributed among sons. In case of no male issue, the half of property is distributed to those daughters who were married through *khandariya* (service). Eldest son succeeds the authority in the family. Though women assist the men in day to day economic activities, they have low status. Their job is to collect fuel, roots and tubers, bring potable water, participate in social function and religious performance. They participate in economic activities. They also contribute to family income by doing labour work.

Women observe certain taboos during pregnancy to ward off evil eye. Earlier, elderly female member of the family attended to the task of delivery with the help of their own *suyarin* (locally trained midwife). Sometimes they also take the help of a Varli *suyarin*. *Sayarin* prepares the *jholi* (hanging cradle) for the new born. *Pansuthi* is the first post-birth ritual. Both the mother and the child are given bath and the newborn is ceremonially placed in *jholi*. *Chhathi* is performed on the sixth day when *kur* deities are worshipped and mother herself names the child. *Babri* (tonsure) is performed on the male child by the maternal uncle one year after birth. A girl, in her first menses, is confined for three days when she cannot enter the kitchen. *Ramram* and *maibap* (negotiation) for marriage is initiated by boy's father with the help of his wife's brother. *Bol-ghan / pend-bharti* (betrothal) takes place one month prior to *lagin* (marriage) at the bride's residence. *Pend* (bride price) in kind is paid to the bride's father and date of *barhard* or *lagin* (marriage) is fixed. Marriage ceremonies last for three days and the ritual starts with the installation of *mandav* (marriage booth) and worship of *kur* deity. *Harad* (turmeric mixed with groundnut oil) is rubbed on the bodies of both one day before marriage at their respective houses. Marriage can be solemnised at either of the houses which depends on the economic condition. In case of *khandaria*, marriage is solemnised at the bride's residence. If bride's side is economically weak, marriage is solemnized at the groom's residence. *Barhardi* (marriage procession) arrives in bride's or groom's village on third day where they are provided *uttara* (resting place). The groom in his traditional dress, called *pichoda*, is carried to the *mandva* at the bride's house on the shoulders of any one of his relatives. The bride is also brought to *manduva*. A knot is tied between the garments of the both. Both the bride and the groom circumambulate five times round the *umar* tree, installed in *mandva*, to perform *fera* in the midst of the verses recited by *bhagat* (priest). The groom ties *ganthi* (marriage pendant) round the neck of the bride. Brothers of the both lift them on their shoulders and dance, concluding the rituals. The groom with his bride and *varhardi* returns to his village next morning. Consummation of marriage takes place at the groom's residence. The principal ceremony connected with marriage is the tying of *ganthi*. She is called by her parents after five days. Bridegroom, his father and mother visit the bride's village after five days and bring her back to their village. Traditionally they bury their dead. Economic condition is one of the reasons for burying, as cremation is more expensive, since it involves purchase of wood and kerosene oil. Eldest son acts as the chief of mourner. Turmeric paste is applied on hands, feet and face and clothes are changed before burying. Women also accompany the funeral procession upto the village boundary. A stone memorial is erected on the burial site in the name of deceased. Toddy and *daru* are served to the party members on their return from burial. *Daharo* is performed after the completion of one month to remove death pollution by the *bhagat* of the Kokna or Varli. *Kur* members are called and *daru* is served. They throw cooked rice on the roof of their houses every year on Diwali in the name of the departed soul.

Forest is their major resource. Tanning of the dead animals' skin is their traditional occupation. They take out the hide of dead animals and sell it to the Chamar. Labour in agriculture and forest is their other present day primary occupation. Women work as maidservants. Basket and *mad* (honey) making are their other means of livelihood.

They make *sunppa* (winnowing fan), *tokra* (basket) of bamboo, *tatki* (mat) which they sell or exchange with rice in the *adhwaras* (weekly local market) at Silvasa and Dudhni village. They also sell the baskets in cash e.g. a *sunppa* costs rupees seven and *tatki* rupees two per feet. A labourer engaged by the forest department, receives his wage in cash. A labourer working in agriculture, receives his wage in both cash and kind i.e. rupees five and one time food or one *athwa* which includes two kg of paddy and one time meal. They also have the system of *baradhi* where they bring the cattle from the Rajput, look after them for four months and in return they get 32 *piali* of *bhat* (rice) and *nagli*. The landlessness among the Koli Dhor has caused the unemployment of daily wager and agricultural labour who temporarily migrate to the neighbouring areas of Gujarat and Maharashtra for three to five months after and before *chaumasa* (rainy season).

Traditionally social control is exercised by the two tier system of *karbhari* (tribal head of village) and Patil (tribal head). Being the hereditary post the tenure of a *karbhari* or a Patil remains life long. The *karbhari* takes care of the daily activities and disputes over cattle, land, divorce and adultery in the village. If he fails in solving the disputes the Patil is approached. Cash fine and drink party are the forms of *kadi mudi* (punishment) imposed by the Patil. In changing situation their political structure has weakened and they approach to the Patil of the Kokna and Varli who dominates the village. Planning and implementation of development programmes are the roles of modern statutory panchayat and has got nothing to do with the disputes.

They profess tribal religion and their belief and practices are associated with the totemic objects and their spiritual power. Hirwa Deo, Khandva, Chitoba, Mai Devi and Kansari Devi are their kul deities. Vagh Deo (tiger god) and Gam Devi are their village deities who are worshipped once in a year where *sindur* (verrmillion) is applied and a goat is sacrificed. The ritual is performed by the Kokna or Varli *bhagat*. The Koli Dhor simply witness the rituals and get their due share after sacrifice. Makar dev (deity of harvesting) and Mawali are the other deities. They also worship Mahadeo and Uma, the deities of wider pantheon. *Bhagat* (religious specialist) officiates at their life cycle rituals and exorcises the evil spirit during the illness. They also call the *bhagat* of Kokna and Varli to pacify the *bhutar* (ghost). Their major festival is Shun and fair is Holi held at Lavacha. They also celebrate the other Hindu festivals namely Diwali, Holi, Akhateej. The community also have the Christian converts and followers of Jalaram sect but the old practice still continues. Their art is represented by the craft of making baskets. The products are *sunppa*, *tokra* and *takki* which are made of bamboo, toddy and palm tree procured from the forests. *Tarjawana* (tattooing) and *chalu* (folk dance) are the non-materialstic object of culture which are enjoyed by both the men and women.

They maintain traditional linkages with the Chamar for the supply of skin of the dead animal and with the Parsi and Rajput for rendering agricultural labour. They take the services of *bhagat* from the Varli and Kokna for the worship of the village deities and also at the time of delivery. Having been placed in the lowest social hierarchy, they accept water, *sidha*, *pucca* and *kachha* food from all the communities. The custom of *baradhi* is maintained with the Rajput. They have their own crematorium and burials. They share their well and temples with the Kokna and Varli. Cultivator-labour relationship is maintained with the Parsi and Rajput and with the landowners in the neighbouring areas of Gujarat and Maharashtra. They participate with the Kokna and Varli in the Holi fair at Lavacha. They also have teachers among them.

They have a positive attitude towards the developmental programmes. The literacy has gone up. Boys study upto secondary level and drop out due to econnomic reasons. They have to support their family. Girls do not study due to poverty. They make use of both the old and the modern medicare. They avail of the facilities of primary health centre. Though they favour family planning programme, they prefer to have four children. Rivulets and dug wells are their drinking water resources. They avail of the facilities of right of conservation under social forestry where they are allowed to cut one bundle of forest wood to use as fuel. They make use of free electricity. They avail of the facilities of animal husbandry under IRDP, mid-day meal for children and mother-infant care through Anganwadi under ICDS and public distribution system. Firewood and kerosene oil are the means of fuel for them. They are exposed to mass communication through cinema, road. Though they are poor, they try to depend on their own resources. But during festive occasions in order to procure necessary household goods, they need financial help for which they have to depend on *sauhar* (moneylender) and shopkeepers.

N.K.Sinha

REFERENCES

Ballal K.D., *Dapada : A village in Dodra and Nagar Haveli*, Census of India, '71, Govt. of India Press, Delhi, Series Part VI-C, 1974.

Enthoven R.E., *Tribes and Castes of Bombay* Vol. II, 1920, Bombay, The Government Central Press, Reprint, Vol. II, p. 253, 1975, Cosmo Publications, Delhi.

Census of India, 1971, *General Economic, Social and Cultural tables*, Series 27, Part III-A & B and Part IV-A,, Delhi, 1974.

MAKRANA

The Makrana are a Muslim community. According to their legend they were brought from Makran in Baluchistan (presently in Pakistan) by the then ruler of Dharampur State Mahadeoji to serve as soldiers. They were deployed in the services of Naroli State from Dharampur, one of the subedars of Dharampur ruler. The Makrana were provided land in the village of Randha, Vanta, Shailly and Markhal against their services after the Portuguese occupied the area. They perceive their distribution in the said villages of the Union Territory. Somehow they are also distributed in Pardi and Dharampur talukas of Gujarat and Khandesh of Maharashtra. Makrani is their spoken dialect which is similar to Baluchi and script is Arabic.

They are also conversant with Gujarati and Urdu and use Gujarati script, while dealing with others. They are non-vegetarian and take egg, fish and meat of goat and fowls.Their staple food includes wheat, rice and pulses of *tur* and *mag* (green gram). *Khajur* was their traditional food item which they left after they came to India. They also consume locally available seasonal fruits and vegetables. Alcoholic drinks are strictly prohibited and they take only non-alcoholic drinks viz. tea, milk and butter milk. They are fond of smoking cigerattes and chewing betel. *Biriyani* (fried rice with mutton) and *zarda* are their special dishes for the festive occasions.

The Makrana include themselves in the Baluchi group of the Sheikh category of Muslim social stratification. They are known as Baluchi in Dharampur and Khandesh. The community name is based on territorial differentiation. They suffix Sheikh to their names which is a post independence phenomenon. They consider themselves inferior to the Rajputs, Brahmin, Kapadia, Parsi, Agri, Bharward, Kahar, Dhodia and superior to the Dubla, Varli, Kokna, Koli Dhor, Kathodi and Chamar. They marry within the community and the rule of exogamy is applied to the extent that a boy and a girl do not have breast feeding from the same mother. Though consanguineous marriage i.e. both the parallel and cross cousin marriages are permitted, it is an intersting feature to note that in reality they do not practise consanguinity. They practise adult marriage and the age at marriage for a girl ranges from eighteen to twenty years while for a boy from twenty to twenty two years. Marriage is settled through negotiation only. They allow monogamy and polygyny both sororal and non-sororal marriages but they practise monogamy only. They conceive that the present economic condition does not allow to go for polygynous marriage. Marriage with wife's sister is allowed after wife's death. *Dagina* (mehr) is fixed during *sagai* (betrothal) and fifty percent of *dagina* is paid during *nikah* (marriage) and remaining fifty percent is promised to be paid in future. A girl, after marriage goes to stay with her in-laws. *Talak* (divorce) is granted to men only in presence of Mukhi (chief of traditional council). If woman desires a divorce, she approaches the Mukhi, who solves the issue, trying to bring about a compromise with her husband. One has to pass through *iddat* period to ascertain if wife has conceived or not. During this period both husband and wife live separately. After the *iddat* period it is again ascertained by the Mukhi whether they desire to have divorce. If they do, *talak* is given in the presence of two witnesses, by uttering the word '*talak*' three times, and wife is free. The amount against *dagina* is paid to the woman. Children become the responsibility of father. The reason for divorce are maladjustment and cruelty. They do allow remarriage to widow, widower and the divorce which takes place as per the Muslim *Shariyat*.

Their family institution is of extended type. Eldest member of the family is paid due respect. Avoidance relationship is maintained between mother-in-law and son-in-law, father-in-law and daughter-in-law, with younger brother's wife and husband's elder brother. Married women cover their head in front of avoidance relatives. They use *burqa* (cloak) while going out of their houses. Joking relationship is maintained with elder brother's wife, husband's younger brother and wife's brother's and sister's. Conflict arises after son's marriage and father's death on financial matters. Women also have right of inheritance. Fifteen percent of the property goes to the daughter, twenty five percent to the widow mother and remaining sixty percent is equally shared by the sons. After mother's death, her property goes to the son who has looked after her, or she can make her own will during her life time. Eldest son succeeds to the authority. Inter-family linkages can be sought during the life cycle rituals, in economic activities and during the election of *jamat* Mukhi (traditional council chief). A Makrana woman has low status. Her role is restricted to the household jobs and rituals. She also has to collect fuel-wood and bringing potable water.

The expectant mother has to observe certain restrictions during her pregnancy to avoid miscarriage. She is expected to carry a knife or a piece of iron to protect her foetus and is not alllowed to go out in the night, specially during full moon. *Showver* is the pre-birth ritual performed in first pregnancy and thereafter the expectant mother goes to her parents. Elderly female member of the family attends the delivery. The new born child first of all hears the *takbir* (prayer), said to the creator. Father or any other elderly member of family then repeats the prayer in the ear of the newborn. This is called *azan* (call). The first purificatory bath of mother and child takes place on the sixth day after birth. The child is named by the father or grandfather with the help of Koran. The father opens any page of Koran at random and the first letter of the first word of third line is taken as the initial of the child's name. *Agiga* (sacrifice) and *mundan* (tonsure) are performed to both male and female child after the completion of three or four months. *Shunnat* (circumscision) is performed by the *khalifa* eight days after the birth. They observe birth pollution for forty days. The first Ramjan fast of a boy or girl is initiated after the completion of eight years. Marriage negotiations are initiated by boy's parents. *Shagai* (betrothal) takes place fifteen days to one year prior to *nikah* (marriage). Marriage is solemnised at the bride's residence as per the Islamic *Shariyat* (law). The *barat* (marriage procession) arrives in the bride's village where they are given separate lodging. The bridegroom with the *barat* arrives at the bride's house. The principal ceremony connected with *nikah* is recital of *kalma* from their holy book of *namaz* (prayer), and taking groom's and bride's acceptance for the marriage separately - this is done by the *kazi* (priest) three times. The half of the *dagina* is paid by the groom's father to the bride's father. Marriage dinner is given by the bride's parents. The groom with his bride and the *barat* returns to his village next day. Consummation of marriage takes place at the groom's residence. They bury their dead. *Namaze janaza* (funeral prayer) is performed at the gate of the mosque before the funeral procession starts for the burial ground. *Shayum* (recital of Koran Shareef) is performed on the third day to remove pollution and for the final send off to the departed soul. *Chalisi* is performed after forty days for the peace of the departed soul and poor, *takeen* (beggers) and religious specialists are fed. The mourning period extends upto six months during which no festivals are celebrated.

Land is their major economic resource. The community has both the landowners and the landless. As discussed earlier, initially the Makranas were engaged as soldiers by the then Dharampur and Nagar Haveli states. Agriculture is their present primary occupation. They now own some land, given to them by the then State for their services; after the Portuguese occupied the region. Their agricultural products are of subsistence level. Their agricultural implements are indigenous and they are mainly dependent on rain. Their crop calendar is divided into three stages namely *siara* (winter) for *tur*, *moong*, and wheat cultivation, *unodu* (summer) for rice and *jowar*, and *chaumasa* (rainy season) for *ragi* and rice. They sell pulses and *ragi* to the Banias at Silvasa. Agricultural labour and industrial labour are other means of their livelihood. They visit Vapi in Gujarat to work as labour in agriculture and industries. Agricultural labourers get their remuneration and during agricultural season they get cash plus one time food.

Social control is exercised by their *jamat* (traditional council) at village level. The *jamat* is headed by a Mukhi (chief) and assisted by five *panchas* (members) who are elected by voice vote. Social problems pertaining to inter-family disputes, *nikah*, *talak*, disrespect to traditional norms and adultery are dealt with by the *jamat*. Disrespect to council and inter-caste marriages are the major social offences and an offender is excommunicated. Plan implementation and welfare and developmental activities are the responsibility of modern statutory panchayat.

They profess Islam and belong to Sunni sect. They have faith in *pir* and visit the *mazar* (memorial tomb) of Jorawar pir located in the Chikhali Taluka of Valsad District in Gujarat to fulfill their promises. Their major shrines are Meeca and Ajmer Sharif at Ajmer in Rajasthan. *Kazi* and *maulvi* are their sacred specialists who perform their life cycle rituals and conduct religious performances. They also have faith in magic and sorcery. Their major festivals are Id-ul-fitr, Id-ul-Joha, Shab-e-barat and Muharram which are associated with the religion. They do not seem to have any artistic traits.

Traditionally, they were linked with the Rajput as soldiers working for them, for which they were brought from Makran. They accept water, *kachha* and *pucca* food from all the Hindus and Christians except the Chamar and Koli Dhors. They have their own burials and mosques.

They share well and water resources with others. Crop sharing relationship exists with the Rajputs and Varli. Cultivator-labour relationship exists with the Rajputs, Varli, Dublas, Dhodia and Koli Dhors. Their political leadership has emerged at village statutory panchayat where they have representation.

The literacy level has gone up among the boys who study upto secondary level and drop out from studies due to economic reasons. They have to earn to support their families. Girls are allowed to study only upto primary level in Madarsa and drop out from studies due to the social reasons. They avail of the facilities of health and medicare and make use of both the indigenous and modern medicine. They do not favour family planning and prefer to have four or more children. Drinking water is available to them through dug-wells. They use electricity and organic manure and chemical fertilizer for farming. They get sugar, kerosene oil and rice from the fair price shops. They avail of the facilities of mother infant care under ICDS. They use firewood, cowdung cakes and kerosene oil as fuel. The area where they live has a good network of roads, both metalled and unmetalled, for transportation. Being agriculturists at subsistance level, their savings are less and they have to depend on money-lenders and shopkeepers in their needs.

N.K. Sinha

REFERENCES

Rajyagor, S.B., *Gazetteer of India, Gujarat State, Junagadh District*, Registrar General, Government of India Press, Delhi, 1975.

MAURI RAJPUT

The Mauri Rajput, a warrior class, are from Agni kula (fire born) and trace their origin to the Parmar Rajput of Abugarh. According to a legend the Parmars left Abugarh in 144 A.D. because of some war. The Mauri came to Chittorgarh first and then to Ujjain and Lata (presently Bharooch in Gujarat) and finally to Dharampur State. They came to Nagar Haveli after they were provided the Subedari of 66 villages in return of their services to the ruler of Dharampur in 1783. The ruler of the Mauri Rajputs stayed at Dharampur while others came to Nagar Haveli and Nathu Mauri was the first to settle here. The ruler of Dharampur also gave than the jagir of Budhsar (in Gujarrat) in lieu of their services. Russel and Lal (1975 : Vol. 10-412) has discribed the Mori as Parmars, one of the thirty six great clans of Rajput. Sherring (1974: Vol. II p. 145) and Enthoven (1920 : Vol. III Page-271) stated that the Mori are one of the fourteen branches of Parmar, the Fire race, who had their kingdom at Ujjain, Chittor. The first Chandragupta, contemporary to Alexander the Great, was said to be of the Mori branch. They see their distribution in Naroli, Silvasa and also in Gujarat. Gujarati is their language and script. They also speak Hindi.

They are non-vegetarian who eat fish, meat of goat and fowls. The nonvegetarian dishes are enjoyed on festive occasions. Their staple food includes wheat, rice, *jowar*, pulses of *tur* and *urad*. They use groundnut oil for cooking. They also consume plenty of locally available fruits and vegetables. Only men take alcoholic drinks which they purchase from the market. *Puri* (fried bread), *srikhand* (made of sugar and curd) and *dudh pag* (rice boiled in milk mixed with sugar) are the special food preparations which are made during marriages and other festive occasions. They also take toddy, smoke cigarettes and chew betel.

The Mauri Rajput constitute one of the thirtyfive *shakhas* (branch) of the Parmar clan of Rajput. They claim to be from Vashistha *gotra*.

They are divided into a number of exogamous *kuls* (lineage) out of which only two namely Agri and Dodia could be traced. The basis of differentiation is social. The main function of *sakha* and *kul* is to indicate descent and to regulate marriage alliances. They have started suffixing Parmar in place of Mauri after liberation. They perceive their position inferior only to the Brahman and superior to all other communities in the regional social hierarchy. They are well aware of the varna system and recognise their place in Kshatriya order.

They marry with the Chauhan, Solanki, Gehlot and Rathod. Earlier these Rajput clans were not considered the community as Rajput royal clan. Chauhan and Solanki settled earlier to the Mauri. It was only when Pratham Singh of the community, one of the descendants of Nathu Mauri, interpreted the history of migration and origin from the Parmars of Rajasthan, that other Rajput clans started matrimonial relations with them. The other rules of exogamy are applied to *sakha*, *kul* and village level. Though tradition allows them to go for polygyny but they practise monogamy. They practise adult marriage. Marriage is settled by negotiations only. Self arranged marriage is not permitted and in such cases they go for courtship under changing situation. *Ganthi* (marriage pendant) is tied round the neck of a married woman as her marriage symbol. They have practice of *dej* (dowry) both in cash and kind. The amount of dowry is fixed during negotiation and is paid during *chandla* (betrothal). A girl after marriage goes to stay with her-in-laws. Divorce and remarriage are not permitted by the community.

Their families of are of extended type. Members of the family are expected to pay respect to elderly members. They have prescribed kinship usages viz. avoidance and joking relationships. Avoidance relationship is maintained between daughter-in-law and parents-in-law, with husband's elder brother, and with younger brother's wife. A woman is supposed to cover her head in front of the avoidance relatives. A *bahu* (daughter-in-law) can not talk to her father-in-law directly. Joking relationship is maintained with husband's younger brother, his wife and elder brother's wife, and with wife's brother/sister. Conflict and confrontation, in the family, arise after father's death on property matters. Traditionally, they had a rule of male primogeniture. Now they follow Portuguese Inheritance Act where the widow inherits half of the property and the remaining is equally shared by the sons. Eldest son succeeds the authority in the family. Sister's husband plays the role of *anwar* (accompanier) and mother's brother brings *maushala* (customary gift) in marriage. They believe in living jointly and the extended family still continues. Women have low status. They observe seclusion. They do only household jobs. They have roles in bringing potable water, attend to social functions, and rituals and religious practices. *Fui* (father's sister) plays a role during *botan* (*annaprashan*), *babri* (tonsure) and naming. Sister plays the role in *rakhadi* and as *kureli* (accompanier) to the bride in marriage.

The life cycle rituals of the Mauri Rajput are common to those of the other Hindus of the region due to their long association with the other Hindu communities of Gujarat and the territory. In spite of that they still practise some of the traditional Rajput customs. In the fifth month of first pregnancy the husband's sister ties a *rakhadi* (guardian - thread) round the right wrist of the pregnant woman. Naming ceremony is performed by the father's sister only after finding the *rashinam* (zodiac name) from the Brahman on twelfth day. *Botan* (first feeding of cereals) is performed in fifth or seventh month in case of a girl and in sixth or eighth month in case of a boy. *Dudh- pag* is prepared for the function, and *fui*'s role in the ceremony is important. *Yagno pobit* (sacred thread) ceremony is performed either during *babri* or after ten to fifteen years of age to get acquainted with Hindu *sanskara* (sacrament) and it is at this occasion that a vow of celibracy or *brahamacharya* is taken. A marriage cannot take place if sacred thread ceremony is not performed. In marriage a *toran* (a triangle of three wooden bars, having the apex crowned with the effigy of a peacock) is erected at the entrance of the *mandava* (marriage stage). The bridegroom hits his sword on the *toran*, indicating supremacy of eloper and marriage by eloping. After death, mourning is observed for thirteen days for man, nine days for woman and three days for a child and *shradh* is performed. The ritual of offering sacrificial cakes is performed on tenth, eleventh, twelfth and thirteenth day after death. The seven days marriage rituals are now reduced to three days to save time and expenditure. Marriage is solemnised at the bride's residence and consummated at the groom's residence.

Land is their major economic resource. They are a landholding community. Traditionally, they have been warriors and zamindars. As discussed in their history of migration, they were given the *subedari* (feudatory) of Nagar Haveli. As a tradition, they were not engaged in agriculture themselves but were the landlords of 66 villages. In course of time they started cultivation and also gave their lands to the tenants. Presently, agriculture is their primary occupation. They engage agricultural labourers and also do cultivation on *bhagidari* (crop sharing). Production of crops is done on commercial level. They grow rice, *jowar*, pulses of *tur* and *moong*. Horticulture and service in different government offices are other means of their livelihood. They also grow seasonal vegetables and do plantation of fruits like mango and *chiku*. They sell their produces to the Vanias of Vapi who come in contact with them before the harvesting. Fruits and vegetables are directly sold in the market at Silvasa and Vapi. The land tenure system is also prevalent with the Kokna, Dhodia and Dubla where the owner gets one third of the produces. It came down to one sixth after the Land Tenancy Act, 1971 was introduced in the region on 1.5.1974. They also do crop sharing where cultivator's share varies from 40% to 60% but the landowner has to bear the expenditure on seeds and fertilizers. Supply of chemical fertilizer, facilities of electric handpumps for irrigation and good quality of seeds have played an important role in the economy of the Mauri Rajput.

Social control among the Mauri Rajputs is exercised by Mauri Parmar Rajput Panch (traditional caste council) on village level, headed by Pramukh who is elected by voice vote. Pramukh is assisted by a *karbhari* (manager) and five *sabhyas* (members). Being traditionally the ruling class they have tradition of chieftianship which changed after liberation. Growing political awareness among them due to the periodical elections resulted in fractions in the community and they organised a council, for which Pramukh is elected after every five years. The election criteria are the age of the man, his economic status, his popularity among the community and knowledgeability regarding the worldly affairs of the community. The *panch* regulate their daily activities. Social problems pertaining to deviation from the traditional norm, inter-caste marriage, adultery, inter- family and inter- community disputes are dealt with by the Pramukh. Pre- marital and extra-marital relations are considered the biggest offence. In such cases the offender is excommunicated. If a boy marries a girl from other community he is excommunicated and cannot be socially accepted back in the community till he deserts her. Plan implementation, welfare and developmental activities are the responsibility of modern statutory panchayat.

They profess Hinduism. Except local peculiarities, they do not differ from other Hindus of the region in their religious performances and practices. Though many are followers of the Jalaram Sect (a saint from

Gujarat) or Krishanites, or the devotees of Shirdi Ke Sain Baba, they have always been more keen on the worship of Lord Shiva and Amba Mata the community deities as well as village deities. The newly married couple is supposed to pay homage to these deities next day after marriage. *Gotrej* is a term for *kul* deity who is worshipped ceremonially once in a year on *athem* (eight day) of Magh month. They also worship all the Hindu gods and goddesses and their *devsthan* (shrine) at home contain the images of Shiva, Vishnu, Hanuman, Amba and Ganpati. Amba Mata temple in Gujarat and Shiva temple at Palsana in Gujarat are their major shrines. Brahman officiates at their life cycle rituals and religious performances. Their major festivals are Navratra, Athem and Nagpanchami. Amba Mata is the deity of war. Their swords are considered sacred to them and are worshipped during Navratra. Sword worship is also performed during birth and marriage. Shivratree Fair at Palsana in Gujarat is their main fair which is held on Shivratree day. The community does not have any art of their own. *Satiya* (floor design), and folk songs of birth and marriage are common to other Hindus. *Dandi-ras* is the folk dance, which they have borrowed from the Gujarat during their early association with Lata (Bharooch) and Dharampur.

They accept *kachha* food from the Brahman only. They accept water and *pucca* food from the Brahman and Kapadia. They do invite the Kapadia, Agri and Vania in marriage but do not dine with them. The feeling of untouchability still prevails in relation to the Chamar, Koli Dhor and Kathodi. They allow Dubla, Kokna and Dhodia to work in their houses and accept water touched by them. Inter community marriage is not a norm and is generally not allowed. There are, however, a few cases of courtship. They have their own temples, crematoriums and drinking water resources. They participate in the Shivratri fair at Palsana with others. Patron-client relationship exists with the Brahman for rituals and religious performances, with the Chamar for the cleaning of the dead animal and for the services of the Chamarin (Chamar's wife) during birth. Landlord-tenant relationship is maintained with the Makrana, Dhodia and Kokna. Cultivator-labour relationship is maintained with the Dubla, Dhodia and Varli. They participated actively in the liberation movement of the territory. In this connection one of the community members Guman Singh deserves special mention. Naroli was liberated from the Portuguese with his help on 28.7.1954. Presently their political leadership has emerged at regional level where they have representation in modern statutory panchayat. In the community there are scholars, engineers and doctors and others holding white collar jobs.

Their attitude towards development programme is positive. The literacy level has gone up. Boys study upto post-graduate level and start earning. Girls study upto college level and drop out due to social reasons. They make full use of modern medicare. They favour family planning programmes and prefer to have three children. They avail of the facilities of drinking water through tube well and pipes, irrigation through electric tube wells, child and mother care under I.C.D.S. and ration distribution system. They make use of electricity, organic manure, chemical fertilizer and pesticides which they get from the government agencies. Firewood, kerosene oil and L.P.G. are their fuel resources.

N.K. Sinha

REFERENCES

Enthoven,R.E., *Tribes and Castes of Bombay*, Vol. III, 1922, Bombay, The Government Central Press, Reprint, Vol. III, p. 271, 1975, Cosmo Publications, Delhi.

Russell,R.V. and Rai Bahadur Hira Lal, *Tribes and Castes of the Central Provinces of India*, Vol. IV, 1916, London, Macmillan and Company; Reprint, Vol IV, p. 412, 1975, Cosmo Publications, Delhi.

Sherring,M.A., *Hindu Tribes and Castes* Vol. II, 1879, Calcutta, Thakar Spink & Co.; Reprint Vol. II, p. 145, 1974, Cosmo Publications, Delhi.

PARSI

The Parsi are the immigrants from Persia (presently Iran). Their name has been derived from Pars of Faras, a province of Persia whose capital is presently at Shiraz. Parsis are the descendants of those who left Persia during the Arab invasion, due to conversion to Islam by force, sometime in seventh centuary. Karaka (1986), Thornton (1987) and Ballal (1941) support this view. According to legends they boarded a ship and sailed for other places with their Holy Fire and landed first at Diu, then came to Sanjan near Vapi in Gujarat. They were given shelter by Zadi Rana (the ruler of Sanjan) on the request by Meharji Rana, their *dastur* (priest). After the death of Zadi Rana, Sanjan was raided by the Muslim invader and the Parsi left Sanjan and came to Nargol (presently in Maharashtra), Saronda and Dewiyar. From these places they spread to different parts and out of them fifteen families came to the Territory, and Nairoji was the first to settle. They placed their Iranshah (Holy fire) at Udhwada (Gujarat). They are spread in the villages of Dapada, Amboli, Khanvel, Dudhni and Randha. They are also scattered at the different places of Daman, Gujarat and Maharashtra with their main concentration at Surat, Navsaree, Valsad, Bombay and Udhwada. The dispute over the reckoning of the year split the community into two sub groups sometime in the eighteenth century. The sub groups were Shehenshahi (who adopted the Indian practice) and Kadamis (who retained the Persian practice). According to Census of India, 1981, their population in the territory is 26 only. Gujarati is their spoken language as well as their script. The male members put on a headgear peculiar to them. The priests put on white dress. Parsis are a religious minority group.

They are non-vegetarian who eat fish, egg, meat of goat and fowls. Their staple food includes rice, *jowar*, wheat, pulses of *tur* and *urad*. Groundnut oil is their cooking medium. They have good intake of fruits. Men take alcoholic drinks regularly which they purchase from the market. They also take drinks made by the tribals at homes. *Lapsi, dhokla, dudhpag* are the special food preparations of the festive occasions.

The subgroups, mentioned earlier, are divided further into two subdivisions namely Dastur or Attarman (priest class) and Behdin (non-priest class). The Attarman wear white caps while the Behdin wear black caps. The divisions indicate social status and regulate marriages. Their surnames are based on the place and occupation. They consider their position inferior to the Brahman and Rajput. They marry within the community. Traditionally, they were endogamous, being ritually high placed within the community. Now both divisions inter marry. But the Sehanshahi and Kadamis do not inter-marry. They practise adult marriage i.e. the age for a boy is 24 and a girl is 19 years. Marriage is permitted between the sister's children and with the mother's brother's daughter. They have both arranged marriages and *prem-lagna* or love marriage. The approval is usually sought from their parents. Finger ring is the symbol for a married woman. Traditionally, they followed a practice of *samba* (dowry) as mentioned by Ballal (1974) but now, this practice has stopped. A girl goes to stay with her in-laws after marriage. *Chhut-chheda* (divorce) is permissible. Both the man and the woman, seeking divorce, have to live separately for three years. This is to provide time for their reconsideration. If they are still keen on divorce, they approach the *mobid* (chief priest) who calls the parents of the both and grant divorce in the Parsi Matrimonial Court at Bombay or Navsaree. The reasons for divorce are impotancy and no male issue. Post-divorce maintanence is carried by the divorced husband till the women remarries and the amount is fixed by the Matrimonial Court as per the status of the husband. They allow remarriage between a widow and widower and the divorcee, and the marriage takes place at *agyari* (the holy fire temple). Both men and women exchange their rings in the presence of *mobid*. A man can marry his deceased wife's younger sister and his deceased elder brother's wife. Self-arranged and inter-group marriages are the recent development in the community.

Sons prefer to stay separately after marriage. It is father's obligation to look after his daughter in her widowhood or after divorce. Avoidance relationship is maintained between mother-in-law and son-in-law and daughter-in-law and father-in-law. Joking relationship exists with the elder brother's wife, with husband's younger brother and wife's sister's and brothers. As per the Parsi law all sons get equal share in the property after father's death. Conflict and confrontations erupt after father's death on the property matters. Eldest son succeeds the authority in the family. Inter-family linkages are sought during festive occasions, economic activities and social functions like *ghambhar*, six days gathering in a year. Women have low status and their roles are restricted to household jobs. They also attend to social functions and rituals and contribute to family income by doing various jobs.

The life cycle rituals of the Parsi, some of which are common to Hindus because of their association with Zadi Rana of Sanjan, a Hindu ruler, have been discussed in the introduction.

Land is their major economic resource. They are a land owning community. Traditionally they were agriculturists before they left their native country in Persia. Agriculture is also their present primary occupation. Horticulture, trade of timber wood and service in various government and private concerns are other means of their livelihood. Agricultural and horticultural activities are production of crops, fruits and vegetables on commercial level. Their agricultural implements are both indigenous as well as modern. They use tractor for ploughing and electric hand pumps and tubewells for irrigation. The crop calendar is divided into three seasons namely *siara* (winter) for the pulses of *tur* and *moong*, *unadu* (summer) for rice and *jowar* and *chaumasa* (rainy seasons) for *ragi*. They also produce seasonal vegetables and tap toddy. They sell their produces to the Vania of Silvasa, and Vapi and Valsad in Gujarat in cash. They also do the trade of timber, a forest product in the markets of Valsad, Surat, Navsari and Vapi in Gujarat. The land tenure system is also prevalent when they give some of their lands to the Dhodia, Varli and Kokna where they get one third of the produce. They brought the Kathodi from Maharashtra, provided them residential land in their fields and got them to work as *kharchhi-khandel* (bonded labour) in the fields. The Kathodi were freed from bondage only after Abolition of Bonded Labour Act was introduced and they were rehabilitated by the government in 1985-86. The Parsi take the services of the Kathodi, Varli and Dubla as agricultural labour and wages are paid in cash and kind.

Social control is exercised by the traditional council working at three levels. They are *anzuman* at village level *jangal-vasi jarthesth gambhar* at regional level, which includes the Parsi villages of the territory and Parsi Panchayat at Bombay at National level. The Parsi Panchayat is headed by a Pramukh and assisted by a trustee, *karbhari* (representing the each *gambhar*) and members of the executive committee. These office bearers are elected by voice vote. Social problems pertaining to inter-caste marriage and breach of traditional law are dealt with by these councils. The cases of remarriage and divorce are referred to the Parsi Matrimonial Court. An offender is excommunicated. Plan implement and welfare development activities are the role of modern statutory panchayat.

The Parsi profess Zoroastrianism. They worship Agyari (Holy Fire) which they carried from Persia with them to Sanjan and finally placed in their temple at Udhwada in Gujarat. They keep oil lamp burning in their houses which is considered sacred. They carry some of the Hindu religious traits since they were under shelter of Zadi Rana in India, the then king of Sanjan. He put the condition that they adopt some Hindu traits, when he granted them asylum. Accordingly, they make *satiyo* (floor design) on their houses to welcome goddess Laxmi, protect the cows from the Muslims, include Sanskrit verses in marriage rituals, to apply *kanku* (red vermilion mark on the forehead) in marriage, etc. They were given shelter only after *dasturji* (priest) accepted these proposals. According to Ballal (1974), they also have faith in Sitla Devi (a Hindu deity) whom they offer sacrificial goats and fowls and offer oil to Lord Hanuman. They also pay homages to Muslim *pirs*. Atasbedram, the Holi Fire temple at Udhwada is their major sacred centre. *Dasturji* or *mobid* (priest) is their sacred specialist who attends their life cycle rituals and religious cremonies. Only Attarman can become a *mobid* (priest). Their main festival is Puppety. Zend Awastha is their sacred book. Their calendar year is divided into six seasons. They consider the five days viz. Ahunbad, Ustbod, Spentomod, Vahukshtra and Vahistoist as *gatha* (holy days for auspicious festivals). Non-materialistic cultural elements are represented by their folk tales written in the form of verses named Kissaye-Sanjan written by their Dastur Bahman Kakobad Sanjana in 1599. Folk songs of birth and marriage are sung by the female folk only.

They share the occupation of cultivation with Kathodi, Dubla, and Varli. With other communities they have trade relations. They accept water, *kaccha* and *pucca* food from the Rajput, and Kapadia. Though they invite the Agri, Varli, Kokna, Dubla and Dhodia in their marriages, they do not dine with them. They have their own water resources, *agyari* (temple) and *dakhma* (tower of silence where they expose their dead). They participate in the Holi festivals with the Hindu communities.

Patron-client and cultivator-labour relationships exist with the Kathodi, Koli Dhor, Dubla, Varli and Kokna. They have entrepreneur, engineers, doctors as well as some members of the community holdig white collar jobs. Their political leadership has emerged at village panchayats.

Their attitude towards development programme is most favourable. Literacy has gone up both among the boys and girls who study upto post-graduation level. They make full use of modern medicare. They favour family planning programme but prefer to have three children with the use of modern family planning methods. They avail of the facilities of drinking water by dug well and tube well, electrically handled pumps for irrigation, ration distribution system. They make use of electricity, organic manure and chemical fertilizers which they get from Agricultural Department. Fire wood, cowdung cake, kerosine oil and L.P.G. are their fuel resources. Being economically sound, their savings are considerable which they invest in trade. The region has a good network of roads which provides them means of transportation to various places in the Territory as well as in Gujarat and Maharashtra.

N.K. Sinha

REFERENCES

Ballal,K.D., *Depada : A village in Dadra and Nagar Haveli*, Registrar General, Delhi, Census of India, 71, Series 1, Part VI-C:1974.

Karaka, D.E., *History of the Parsi*, Discovery Publishing House, Delhi, Vol. I & II:1986.

Thornton., *Parsi, Jain and Sikh : Some Minor Religious Sections in India*, Mittal - Publication, Delhi:1987.

Census of India, 1981: Series-28, Part A and B, Registrar General, Delhi.

VARLI/WARLI

The Varli, also known as Warla/Warli, are a Scheduled Tribe. Enthoven (Vol-III-445) states that the term Varli is a distortion of *varal* meaning an uplander and may also be derived from *varlat* which is the name of the sixth of the seven ancient Konkans. They do not have any idea about their origin. They presume that they are the original inhabitants of the region. However, Ballal (Census of India, 1971, Part VI-C, page 21) referring to Gazetteer of Bombay (1901) says that the Varlis probably migrated from North Konkan. They are divided into two endogamous divisions, based on religion, namely the Varli and the Christian Varli. They perceive their distribution in sixty villages of the territory. They are also spread in Gujarat and Maharashtra. Their total population according to Census of India, 1971, is 41,071, being the largest tribe in the territory. Varli and Dabar are their spoken dialect and script is Devanagari. They are also conversant with Gujarati especially in their dealings with others. The traditional dress for men is loin cloth and a handcloth for women over the shoulder and round the waist. Now they also wear *choli* (blouse).

Bio-anthropological information is available on the basis of the studies carried out by Joshi et al. (1978) and has been given in Appendix I. They are non-vegetarian who eat the meat of goat, *lawi* (a bird), *shashla* (rabbit). They also take dry fish and land crabs. Their staple food includes rice, *nagli*, pulses of *tur* and *urad*. They use groundnut oil for cooking. They also consume roots, viz. *terri*, *tumou* and tubers viz. *kodukan*, *jeri*, *lunda* and tender bamboo sprouts which they collect from forest. They are very fond of drinking toddy and *daru* (alcoholic drinks). They smoke *bidi* and cigarette. They make *bidi* themselves with tobacco and leaf of *sunghai*. *Shavele*, *khichri* (boiled rice and pulse) and *kanji* (gruel) of *jawar* or *nagli* are their special food preparation made during wedding and other festivals.

The two endogamous divisions of the Varli are further divided into about hundred of exogamous divisions. The *kurh* (clan), namely Dumbhara, Kurhada, Mangiya, Kakwa, Dhinde, Kalanghra, Dodia, Putkar, Bhanwar, Dongorkar, Vartha, Kanat, Andher, Wadvi, Januthya, Dhargrha, Kharpadiya, Khurat, Thalker, Varhagya, Mor etc. are based on the totemic objects. The basis of differentiation is social and occupational. They suffix these *kurhs* to their names. Recently they have also started suffixing Vaidya and Shah to their names. The main function of *kurh* is to trace descent, and to regulate marriage alliances. They are not aware of varna system. They consider their position inferior to the Brahman, Rajput, Kapadia, Agri, Kahar, Parsi, Bharwad, Dhodia, Dubla and Kokna and superior to the Makarana, Chamar, Kothodia and Koli Dhor.

They allow marriage with the father's sister's daughter. A man can marry her wife's younger sister after her death, or even in her lifetime with her consent, if the first wife is barren. Traditionally, they had practice of child marriage followed by *ana*. Presently they practise adult marriage and the age at marriage for a boy ranges from eighteen to twenty years and for a girl from fourteen to ninteen years. Marriage is settled by negotiation, *ghar-mani* (son-in-law stays at bride's place), mutual consent and *khandariya* (marriage by service). The mode of *khandariya* is practised by the Varli who cannot pay the *dej* (bride-price) and has no land. He serves at the bride's village for a stipulated period of three to five years and marries the girl. If he desires, he can return to his village after marriage or stay at the bride's village and become the *jamai* (son-in-law) of the village. If he stays with his bride's parents, he is called *ghar jamai*. In this form of marriage all expenditure in marriage is borne by the bride's parents. A man can keep a girl as his wife without any ritual performences except that he has to provide a drink party to the traditional council for a formal approval. *Dej* (bride price) is paid both in cash and kind. The cash amount ranges from rupees three to four hundred while the kind includes two *mund* of *bhat* (paddy) and five *piyali* (an unit of measurement which contains four kgs. of cereals) of *kathor* (pulses). A married woman ties *ganthi* (marriage pendant, with two beads of aluminium) around her neck as her marriage symbol. *Sorh-chhithee* (divorce) is granted to both man and woman by the traditional council. The reasons for divorce are adultery, barrenness, insanity, witchcraft and sorcery. *Dawa* (repayment of bride price) is demanded by the man from his wife at divorce if she is proved to indulge in extra-marital relationship. If a woman seeks divorce due to insanity of her husband, her husband's party cannot demand *dawa*. Extra-marital relations are not rare among them and if a woman runs away from her husband and stays with her paramour, *dawa* is claimed by the husband. The reunion with other man in society is approved and termed as *natra* (remarriage) in which no *dej* is claimed. The former husband breaks the *ganthi* from her wife's neck during the divorce in the presence of *samaj* (traditional council) and gives up claim over the woman. During *natra* a drink party is given to the father of the divorced or widowed woman and the council. No *ganthi* is tied in *natra*. If an unmarried girl runs away with a boy from other community she is excommunicated. Cases were reported where the Parsi kept a Varli girl as *gharad* (concubine) for years and left her after providing land. She was allowed *natra* from the same community after providing a feast to the *samaj*. There no are separate marriage rules for the Christian Varli except that they practise endogamy. The increase in their marriage age and inter-tribal marriage between the Christian converts of Varli and Kokna, based on *dabra* (love marriage) are recent development.

They have both extended and nuclear types of family. The prescribed kinship usages viz. avoidance and joking are maintained. Avoidance relationship is maintained up to the extent that one cannot cut jokes with whom she or he observes avoidance. Brother has to look after his sister in her widowhood and in case of her divorce. A *khandar* (son-in-law) is also included in family in case of *khandaria* marriage. Maternal uncle has an important role to play during *babri* (tonsure) and the brothers, during marriage. Conflict and confrontation arise in the family on property matters after father's death. A widow inherits half of the property of her husband and the remaining half is equally shared by the sons. In case of no male issue half of the property is shared by the daughters who are married through *khandaria*. Eldest son succeedes the authority. Though women assist the men in day to day life, they have low status. They have roles in collection of fuel, bringing potable water, social function, economic activities and religious practices. They also contribute to family income after doing labour-works and doing teaching jobs.

The lifecycle rituals are common to both the endogamous divisions except that the Chiristian Varli visit the father of church for seeking his blessing after birth and marriage. This has already been discussed in the Introduction.

Land and forest are their major economic resources. They have, among them, both the landowners and landless categories. Land is controlled under individual proprietorship. Terrace and settlement cultivation is traditional and continues to be their present day primary occupation. Those who do not have land, cultivate the land of Parsi and Rajput landowners. In return they get one third of the total yields. Before 1954, one third went to the owner under Tenancy Act but after 1954 the share of the landowner is one-sixth. Tools and implements are indigenous. They mainly depend on rain water for irrigation. They sell their produces in the local market in exchange of both the cash and the kind. Labour job in agriculture, forest, and industries, service in various government offices and *mad* (honey) making are other means of their livelihood. They also worked as *kharchi-khandel* (bonded labour) of the Parsi and Rajput. Though they are poor and try to depend upon their own income, sometimes they have to borrow money for consumer goods, festivals and are supposed to clear their debts within six months failing which, they have to work in the fields of the creditor. Sometimes failure in paying the debt makes them mortgage the land to the creditor. Children and women also work as labourers. There is an increase in the number of agricultural labourer and they visit neighbouring districts of Maharashtra for jobs. An agricultural labour receives his remuneration in cash as well as two *seers* of paddy of *nagli* and one time food or three *seers* of paddy with one time food and cash. Women and children who work on fields get their remuneration in cash. Those who work as forest and casual labourers receive rupees nine and ten.

The *samaj* (traditional council) functions at two levels namely at *parha* (hamlet) level headed by a *karbhari* and at village level headed by a Patil. They are elected by voice vote and the tenure changes every year. Patil is elected by the *karbhari* of each *parha*. The *karbhari* takes care of the daily activities and disputes over cattle, land, divorce, bride price, adultery and remarriage at hamlet level. If *karbhari* fails to resolve issues, the Patil is approached. Cash fine and drink party are the form of *kadi-mudi* (punishment) imposed by the *karbhari* or Patil. Minor criminal assaults are also resolved by the council. They also approach the Sarpanch of statutory panchayat for solving inter-tribal and intra-tribal disputes. An offender is excommunicated by the *samaj*. He/she can be taken back in the community after he/she provides a feast. Even their Patil is considered to be an authoritarian to give his mandate, during the periodical elections of statutory panchayat and parliament.

modern statutory panchayat.

They profess tribal religion and Christianity. Their belief and practices are associated with the totemic objects. Hirwa Dev, Pitar, Nirbhashi, Khandra, Chitobanai and Himai Devi are their clan deities who are worshipped during life cycle rituals, Diwali and Holi. Gam Devi and Wagh Dev are their village deities who are worshipped once in a year on Krishnapaksha Duadshi (twelfth day of the dark half) in Ashwin month when *sindur* (vermillion) is applied and goat is sacrificed. Worship of the village deities is the job of Patil while the *bhagat* does the ritual part of sacrifice. Kansari Devi (deity of grain) and Maker Devi (deity of harvesting) are the other deities. Narsingh Dev is a symbolic deity. Mahodeo is the deity of wider pantheon. Christian Varli visit the church to attend the mass as per their convenience but they also believe in tribal deities and *bhagat*. *Bhagat* officiates at their life cycle rituals and exqrcises the evil spirits during the illness and pacify the ghost. *Shun* is their major festival. Their major fair is Holi fair held at Lavacha. They also celebrate the Hindu festivals viz. Holi, Diwali and Akhateej. The element of art is represented by the Varli wall paintings, *tarjuana* (tattooing), folk songs of harvesting and folk dances. The folk dances are *bhowada* (masks of *bhowada* made of *pangura* wood and *samar* wood), *torpa* (after plantation of paddy) and *dhol* (during Holi). Folk songs are sung by both the men and women. Both participate in *bhowada* and *torpa* dances while only men participate in *dhol* dance. They use *tarpa* (made of pumpkin and bamboo) and *chang* (made of bamboo) like wind instruments and *dhol* (made of sagwan wood and goat skin), the percussion musical instrument with the help of *kadi* (drum beatter).

They accept water, *kachha* and *pucca* food from the Rajput, Brahman, Agri, Kokna and Dhodia. They accept *sidha* from all the communities except the Chamar, Koli Dhor and Kathodi. Inter-community marriage takes place between Christian converts from the Varli and Kokna. The Parsi being the landowners used to take the girls from the Varli. The union was not taken seriously by the community. They share water sources and crematorium with the Kokna. They participate in the Holi fair and marriage ceremonies of others. Job relations are maintained with the Kokna. Landlord-tenant and cultivator-labour relationship exist with the Parsi and Rajput. They have teachers and their political leadership has emerged at village panchayat.

They have a positive attitude towards government's development programmes which include the tribal sectoral programmes. Their literacy level has gone up where boys study upto college level and drop out as they have to earn to support their family. Girls study upto secondary level and drop from studies due to social reasons and they also earn to support their families. They make use of both the indigenous traditional and modern medicare. They avail of the facilities of health and family welfare but prefer to have four or more children. They, however, make use of modern family planning method. Rivulets and dug wells are their drinking water resources. They get the assistance in animal husbandry, poultry, tiles for roof construction under IRDP. They make use of electricity. Fuelwood, firewood and kerosene oil are their fuel resources. They get fire wood through Right of Conservation under social forestry where they are allowed to cut one bundle of wood per day for their fuel consumption. They get organic manure and chemical fertilizers through Agriculture Department. They avail of the facilities of mid-day meal scheme for the children in Balwadi, mother-infant care under ICDS and ration distribution system. They are exposed to mass communication and have been in touch with political parties, extension agencies and voluntary agencies like Vanvasi Kalyan Ashram at Khanvel, Adivasi Social Service Society and Industrial Association Society. They are not sound economically and they need financial assistance during festive occasions for which they have to depend on *sauhar* (moneylenders) and shopkeepers.

N.K.Sinha

REFERENCES

Ballal, K.D., *Dapada: A village in Dadra and Nagar Haveli*, Registrar General of India, Delhi, Census of India 1971, Series I, Part VI-C, 1974.

Enthoven, R.E., *Tribes and Castes of Bombay*, Vol. III, 1922, Bombay, The Government Central Press; Reprint, Vol. III, p. 445, 1975, Cosmo Publications, Delhi.

Malhotra, R. and Mandal, S.K., 'Varli of Gujarat A profile', *Tribe*, Vol XV 11-27, p. 27-40:1983.

Malhotra, R. *et al.* 'Agririan Stratification among the Varli of Gujarat: An observation', *Tribe*, Vol XVI, 3-4:1984.

Save, K.J., *The Varli*, Padma Publication Limited, Bombay:1945.

Appendix

A BIO-ANTHROPOLOGICAL NOTE

In Dadra and Nagar Haveli territory bio-anthropological information is available only for three tribal communities viz. Dhodia, Kokna and Warli.

The phenotype frequencies of ABO blood groups indicate that phenotype A_1 is more predominant among the Kokna 39.28% than in the Dhodia 31.35% and the Warli 24.00%. The freuency of phenotype A_2 is predominant among the Dhodia 2.50% than the Kokna 2.35% and the Warli 1.49%. The frequency of phenotype O is highest in the Dhodia 41.25% and lowest in the Kokna 26.19% whereas the frequency of phenotype B is very low in the Dhodia 20.00% and in the Warli and Kokna frequency of B phenotype is 31.40% and 28.57% respectively.

The Phenotype frequencies of MN system shows that phenotype N is higher than phenotype M among the Dhodia and Kokna whereas there is little difference between M and N phenotype frequencies in the Warli.

For Rh system incidence of phenotype R_1 is highest in the Dhodia 71.25% than in the Warli 64.92% and the Kokna 60.71%. The Kokna has very low frequency of phenotype R_1 R_2 4.76% than the other two tribal groups.

The phenotype frequency of P_1 is lower in the Dhodia 52.50% as compared to the Warli 72.38% and the Kokna 69.5%, whereas phenotype frequency of P_2 is lowest in the Warli 27.62% as compared to the Dhodia 47.50% and the Kokna 30.95%.

The phenotype frequency of secretor varies from 82.01% in the Warli to 79.31% among the Dhodia and 76.46% in the Kokna.

G-6-PD deficiency is found to be quite high in the Warli 19.62% than in the Dhodia 6.35% and the Kokna 8.82%. Colour blindness frequency ranges between 2% to 4% and thalassemia frequency ranges between 2.3% to 3.6% among the three tribes. Individuals having abnormal haemoglobin S are found to be very high among the Dhodia 21.54% and in the Warli 19.53% but lowest in the Kokna 3.61%. The incidence of

Gm^1 is very low in all the three tribal groups, the lowest is in the Dhodia 33.33% as compared to the Warli 59.00% and the Kokna 63.33%. H^p 2-2 phenotype is slightly higher in the Warli 83.19% and H^p o-o type is slightly higher in the Kokna 2.66%.

The three tribal groups viz. the Warli, the Dhodia and the Kokna shows characterstic genetic profile with low frequency of Rh negative phenotype, high frequency of phenotype N and an absence of antigen In^a as well as low frequency of Gm^1. All the three tribal groups possess abnormal haemoglobin S in varing range together with the thalasemic and G-6-PD deficiency trait. Besides these characterstics each tribal group shows distinct features between them. The Dhodia distinguish themselves from other two tribal groups by having high frequency of phenotype O, very low frequency of traits P^1 and Gm^1 high frequency of Hp^1 and moderate frequency of G-6-PD deficiency and higher incidence of HbS. The Warli shows highest frequency of phenotype B and HbS moderate frequency of R. Gm^1 is highest among the Kokna as compared to the Warli and the Dhodia. HbS though present but is in very low frequency in the Kokna.

The three tribal groups are also distinct from each other on the basis of their ethnic and linguistic background wherein the Dhodia are Gujarati speaking and the Warli as well as Kokna are Marathi speaking. The intermixing between these groups is practically absent. The area of the Dadra and Nagar Haveli is hyperendemic for malaria. Due to this these three tribal groups maintained the higher frequency of phenotype Hbs and G-6-PD because of selective resistance to malaria infection and mortality.

Gopal Krishan

REFERENCE

Joshi, S.R., M.M. Mehta, D.M. Mehta, J.P. Bapat, A.J. Baxi and H.M. Bhatia, "Genetic studies in three tribal groups of Dadra and Nagar Haveli region in Western India", *Indian-Journal of Physical Anthropology and Human Genetics*, 4(2), 1978, pp. 133-140.

GLOSSARY

agyari : holy fire temple of the Parsi
agyawan: leader
aqiqa: sacrifice
ana : return of the bride
anjuman: traditional council of the Parsi
anjurhi: homage
anwar: the person who accompanies the groom
asana: Brielia spinusa
atham: eighth day
auna: return of the bride
azan: prayer call
babri: tonsure
babul: Accacia tree
bahu: daughter-in-law
bandi: tunic
baradhi: cattle rearing by way of tenancy
barat: marriage procession
barmal: exchange of garlands in marriage
barshi: memorial rite
bed utary: remarriage
bhagat: priest
bhagidari: share cropping
bhajya: a food preparation
bhat: paddy
bhateda: priest
bhenkar: deer
bhowada: a folk dance

bhowada: mask
bhutar: ghost
bidi: country cigarette
biriyani: fried rice with mutton
bithi chandla: betrothal
boldhan: betrothal
barahadi: marriage procession
botan: first feeding of cereals
boul: wild cat
brahmacharya: bachelor
burqa: cloak
chakmak: lighter
chalisi: fortieth day performance of funeral rites among the Makrana
chang: flute
chap: a type of trap for fishing
chamarin: Chamar's wife
chandla: betrothal
chang: bamboo flute
chhathee pujan: post birth sixth day ritual
chaumasa: rains
chauri: square
cheda: memorial stone
chiku: sapota, a fruit
chola: a dance form
choli: blouse
choly: a dance form
chhutta: divorce
chhutt-chheda: divorce
dagza: a waist coat without sleeves
dakhma: tower of silence, the place for the disposal of dead body of the Parsi
dagina: mehr
dambora: *Conocarpus lati falia*
dandiya ras: a dance form

daru: liquor
dastur: Parsi priest
datedy: sickle
dawa: claim
day: wooden spoon
dej: bride price
dej: dowry
devsthan: shrine
dhamy: a tree
dhokla: a food preparation
dhol: drum
dharko: blouse
diyan: armlet
dorza: anklets
dudh-pak: a sweet preparation
eliyan: armlet
fakir: saint
fenta: headgear
fera: circumambulance
fui: father's sister
gagri: anklet with jingling small bells
Ganpati: Elephant god
ganthi: marriage pendant
garba: dance form
ghàgra: petticoat
ghambar: Parsi annual religious gathering
ghanghori: rain coat
ghangli: a type of jingle bell used in dancing
ghanti: hand grinder
ghard/gharad: concubine
ghar jamai: son-in-law stay at parent's of bride
gharmaoni: concubine
godhely: tattooing
gotrej: clan deity

gotar: chan
granthi: necklace
griha santak: worship of clan deity
gurh: jaggery
hal: plough
hansli: collar, an ornament
har: necklace
harad: worship of clan deity
harad: turmeric
hast milap: joining of hands of bride and groom
hat: local market
hedu: Nanclea cardifolia
hola: dove
iddat: transitory period in divorce among the Muslims
jamai: son-in-law
jamat-mukhi: traditional council chief of the Makrana
jan: marriage procession
jangal-vasi-jarthosth: regional council of the Parsi
janiwas: separate lodging
jeri: a type of tuber
jholi: cradle of cloth
jhori: cradle of cloth
jhulakiyan: ear ring
jowar: millet
kachha: raw food
kachwar: a food preparation
kada: armlet
kadi: drum beater
kado: bracelets
kahadi: a type of flute
kalma: marriage verse from Koran
kanji: a food preparation, gruel
kanku: red mark on forehead
Kansari Devi: deity of grain

kanthi: marriage pendant
kapad: bodice
kasi: a food preparation
kath: catechu
kathod: skin cleaner
karal: harrow
karbhari: manager
kazi: priest of the Makrana
kanyadan: handing over of bride
Kapadi samaj: Kapadia caste Council
kathor: pulses
khaddar: handloom
khalifa: chief
khandar: person married by service
khandariya: marriage by service
kharchhi khandel: bonded labour
khajur: palm
khichri: boiled rice and pulse
khunti: hanger
kodekan: a type of tuber
kodala: hoe
kodukan: a type of tuber
kuhadi: axe
kul: clan
kurh: clan
kurta: shirt
kureli: accompanier to the bride in marriage
lal khair: Acasica sundra
lawi: a bird
lapsi: a sweet preparation
langota: loin cloth
lugda: local sari
lunda: a forest animal
machhi-tadi: negotiation

madaido: a big trap made of reeds
mag: green gram
Makar Dev: deity of harvest
malai: fishing hook
mandva: marriage booth
mandav muhurta: erection of marriage booth
matla: earthen pitcher
maulavi: Muslim priest
maushala: customary marriage gift
mangal fera: circumambulance of the sacrificial fire
mantra: sacred verse
mazar: memorial tomb
mobid: chief priest of the Parsi
moong: green gram
mudi: ear ring
mukhi: chief
mundan: tonsure
nadga: A small drum with a wooden hollow body
nagli: coarse rice
namaz: prayer
namaje-janaza: funeral prayer
nampari: naming
nath: nose ring
natra: remarriage
nawra: bride groom
nawri: bride
nikah: marriage
pachora: a birth ritual
pagdi: head gear
pagran: chain
palav: loose end of saree
panch: caste council
panchas: members of traditional council
pansuthi: birth ritual

parha: hamlet
patel: head
pati: basket
patil: head
Parsi panchayat: Parsi council
pavdo: shovel
pawalakayan: stringed strands of coin
pawi: flute of bamboo with six holes
pend: bride price
pichoda: marriage dress
pir: Muslim saint
piyali: a unit of measurement
pehramni: gift by the relatives
pavalakyan: necklace
pyjama: trouser
pramukh: chief
prem lagna: love marriage
pucca: cooked food
Puppety: a festival of the Parsi
puri: fried bread
ragi: a type of cereal
rakhadi: concubine
ram-ram: betrothal
ran marghi: jungle fowl
ras: folk dance
rashinam: zodiac name
rashoda: kitchen
ratla: thick bread
sabhyas: members
sagad: a type of drum
sagai: betrothal
samaj pramukh: chief of caste council
samar: toothed harrow
samba: dowry

samaj: traditional council
sami: a kind of tree
sanghai: a tree
sankal: anklet
sankhada: necklace
sanskara: sacrament
sauhar: money lender
seer: a unit of measurement
shakha: branch
shashla: rabbit
Shariyat: Muslim personal law
shavree: broom
shesh: a marriage ritual
showver: delivery room
shayum: reciting of verses from Koran
shradh: ancestor worship
Shun: main tribal festival
shunnat: circumscision
siara: winter
sindur: vermilion
sidha: raw food
sorh-chhittee: divorce
srikhand: a sweetfood preparation
srimant: guarding ceremony before birth
satiyo/satiya: floor design
shovle/shovela: a food preparation
siwana: Omedina urborea, a tree
suin: local midwife
sunghai: a kind of plant
supado: winnowing fan
sur: a type of flute
sarpanch: head of statutory panchayat
sutak: ritual pollution
tad cymbal: a musical instrument

tady: toddy
takeen: begger
talak: divorce
tarjuanu/trajuana: tattooing
tatki: mat
tavi: hot plate
teeri: a type of root
temburi or timro: Diaspyros montana, a tree
tittar: a type of bird
tiwas: Dalbergia ougeinersis, a tree
tokra: basket
tondia: a type of trap
torpa: musical instrument
toran: triangle erected in marriage
tumou: a type of root
tur: a type of drum
tur: red gram
thali: plate
umar: tree stick fixed at marriage booth
unadu: summer season
urad: black gram
uthmada: a death ritual
val: creeper
vali: nose ring
vadha: promises
varal: uplanders
Varalat: sixth of the seven names of ancient Konkan
wang: fishing hook
yajnopovit: sacred thread ceremony
zarda: special food preparation by Muslims

SELECT BIBLIOGRAPHY

Bahadur, K.P., *Castes, tribes and cultures of India*, Vol. III, Ess Ess Publication, New Delhi : 1981.

Ballal, K.D., *Dapada: A village in Dadra and Nagar Haveli*, Census of India, Registrar General of India, Delhi, series I part VI-C : 1974.

Ballal, K.D., *Socio-economic profile of Dadra and Nagar Haveli*, Census of India, New Delhi, series-1, Monograph NV 2 : 1974.

Bhatia, R.C., *On Perpetuating the Original Sin Religious conversions of Adivasis* in Ex-Portuguese pockets), AARSI Publication, Moti Daman, Daman : 1986.

Briggi, W.G., *The Chamars*, Reprint, B.R. Publications, Delhi: 1920.

Campbel, James M., *Hindu castes and tribes of Gujarat*, Vintage Books, Gurgaon Haryana, Vol I & II : 1988.

Census of India 1971 *General economic social and cultural tables*, Series-27, Part III, A & B & part IV-A, Delhi, 1974.

Census of India, 1991 *Final Population Totals*, paper 3 of 1991, India, Series-I, Controller of Publications, Delhi, 1993.

Enthoven, R.E., *Tribes and Castes of Bombay*, Vol. I: 1920, Vol. III, 1922, Bombay, The Government Central Press, Reprint, I & III, 1975, Cosmo Publications, Delhi.

Faquir Chand, *Socio Economic Development of Dadra and Nagar Haveli Since Its Liberation* (1987-88). Administration of Dadra and Nagar Haveli, Statistical Wing, Silvasa: 1987.

Fransisco, Antonio — *Notices-e-Documentas-Para-A Historia De Damao*, Bastora Goa), Vol-III : 1904.

Gazetteer of India — Goa, Daman and Diu, Part II & III, pp. 18, Panaji, 1979.

Gazetteer of India — Gujarat State, *Junagadh District* Registrar General, Delhi, 1975.

Imperial Gazetteer of India, — *Coondapoor to Edwardesabad*, Today and Tomorrow's Publishers, New Delhi, Vol. IX: 1908.

Joshi, S.R., M.M. Mehta D.M. Mehta, J.B. Bapat, A.J. Baxi and H.M. Bhatia — 'Genetic studies on three tribal groups of Dadra and Nagar Haveli region in Western India', *Indian Journal of Physical Anthropological Human Genetics*, 4(2), 1978, pp. 133-140.

Kales, D.N., — *Agri: A socio economic survey*, Asia Publishing House, Bombay: 1952.

Karaka, D.F., — *History of the Parsi*, Discovery Publishers, Delhi, Vol I & II : 1986.

Parmar, Dr. H.N., — 'Ramnagareka Rajavi', (the typed Hindi extract taken from the book which was collected from the Administration of Dadra & Nagar Haveli).

Raghvaiah, V., — *Tribal Revold*, Andhra Rashtra Adimjati Sevak Sangh, Nellore: 1971.

Rajendran, S., — *Census of India, 1981*, part III, Series-27, Dadra and Nagar Haveli, Directorate of Census Operation, Panaji, p. 150, 1988.

Roy Shibarni and S.H.M. Rizvi., — *Dhodia Identity*, B.R. Publication Delhi: 1985.

Russel, R.V. and Rai Bahadur Hira Lal — *Castes and Tribes of Central Provinces of India*, Vol. II, 1916, London: Macmillan and Company; Reprint II, 1975, Cosmo Publications, Delhi.

Sane, K.J., — *The Varli*, Padma Publications Limited, Bombay: 1945.

Shah, P.G., — *Tribal life in Gujarat*, Gujarat Research Society, Bombay : 1964.

Sherring, M.A., — *Hindu Tribes and castes*, Vol. II 1879, Calcutta, Thapar Spinks & Co.: Reprint, Cosmo Publications, Delhi, Vol-II : 1974.

Sinha, N.K., 'Dubla Ethnography, Structure and process', Unpublished report submitted to A.S.I.: 1983'.

The Goa League *Report of the New Administration of the conditions in Nagar Haveli and Dadra before and after the Liberation from Portuguers Colonialism*, Independent Publishing Company, London: 1975.

Thornton, D.M., *Parsi, Jain and Sikh: Some Minor Religious Sections in India*, Mittal Publications, Delhi: 1987.

Thurston, E., *Castes and Tribes of Southern India*, Vol-I : 1909, Government Press, Reprint, Vol I., 1975, Cosmo Publications, Delhi.

MAP OF DADRA AND NAGAR HAVELI

(SHOWING DISTRIBUTION OF THE COMMUNITIES

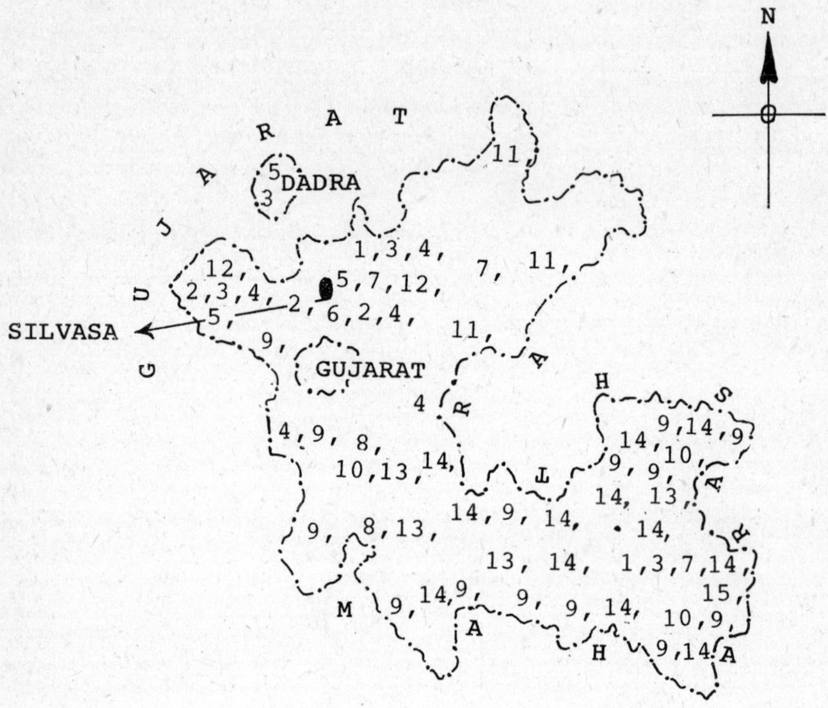

INDEX (NOT TO SCALE)

1. AGRI
2. BHARWAD
3. CHAMAR
4. DHODIA
5. DUBLA
6. KAHAR
7. KAPADIA
8. KATHODI
9. KOKNA
10. KOLIDHOR
11. MAKRANA
12. MAURI RAJPUT
13. PARSI
14. VARLI

INDEX